Billy Soose
The Champion Time Forgot

Rusty Rubin and Tom Donelson

authorHOUSE™

1663 Liberty Drive, Suite 200
Bloomington, Indiana 47403
(800) 839-8640
www.AuthorHouse.com

First published by AuthorHouse 09/16/05

ISBN: 1-4208-6705-9 (sc)

Printed in the United States of America
Bloomington, Indiana

This book is printed on acid-free paper.

Forward: By Rusty Rubin

In May of 2003, I had a visit from Gene Sebastian and his wife May. They had flown from their home in Atlanta, GA. to meet with me in regard to a journalistic endeavor that has resulted in this book.

Gene, the brother of former middleweight champion Billy Soose, had one desire, to keep his word to his dying brother, and see that Billy would be deservedly enshrined in the International Boxing Hall of Fame in Canastota, NY.

While we realized how hard a task that would be, since Billy won the title in 1939, and retired it shortly thereafter, there were many factors that caused me to believe that Billy's being overlooked for induction was a gross miscarriage of justice that must be corrected, and quickly. The problem was obvious, the longer the time passed since he fought, the fewer the people that would remain and remember and give testimony to his greatness.

Billy Soose was on the Hall of Fame ballot for a few years but never received enough votes, maybe it was because few people knew who he was and what he did, and didn't bother to check the record.

Among those who strongly endorse Soose's entry into the International Boxing Hall of Fame are: Hall of Fame trainer Angelo Dundee, historian Hank Kaplan, Hall of Fame Referee Arthur Mercante Sr., and Pennsylvania Athletic Commissioner Greg Sirb.

Noted boxing historian Tracy Calis has this to say: "Billy deserves to be honored in the International Boxing Hall of Fame. Of his six losses, five were to world class fighters- Charley Burley, Jimmy Bivins and Georgie Abrams (3 times). According to "Sugar" Ray Robinson, Abrams was one of Sugar's toughest fights."

Of course, Gene was a great story in himself, a self-made, true unsung American hero, who had served his Country with honor and pride for many years.

This book figured to be a natural, but I also realized that because of time and health constraints I wouldn't be able to undertake the entire task by myself. To that end I asked fellow scribe, outstanding boxing writer Tom Donelson for his help. He did, and I was certainly not disappointed in my choice to co-author this story.

And Tom was able to get even more assistance from talented graphic designer Kim Smith for the cover and an outstanding job of proof reading help by Carol Golden. Also helping with the book design was Scott Sebastian, nephew of Billy Soose.

I believe that Tom Donelson and I have made the case for Billy Soose to get back on the Hall of Fame ballot and for his induction. The rest is left up to the readers and those at Canastota who make up the ballots.

My sincere thanks to all that made this book possible.

Contents

Introduction

Who was Billy Soose, and for that matter, who is Gene Sebastian? I would suspect that even the most knowledgeable of boxing pundits would not be able to answer the questions: So who is Billy Soose?

Billy Soose was one of the top middleweights between 1939 and 1941; whose outstanding ring skills were comparable to even Hall of Fame fighter Tony Zale. A college educated slick boxer, Soose often made his opponents miss and preferred to box from the outside as opposed to engaging in slugfests. This is not to say that he could not go toe to toe, but Soose was an artist in the ring, and his left jab proved to be his paintbrush, with his foes, the canvas. Opponents could not escape the accuracy of Soose's jab.

What made Soose unique was that a hand injury forced him to apply a scientific approach to a sport that often is marked by brutality. Soose was as tough as any fighter of his day; but more often than not, he won his fights with speed and quickness while taking advantage of his 6 feet plus height.

But Soose's uniqueness extended outside the ring. Soose's relationship with his manager, Paul Moss, was one of pugilisms most unusual relationships. Moss discovered Soose in Western Pennsylvania and brought him to the West coast, where Soose began his professional career. Often, even in those days, the manager-boxer relationship was one of the manager or promoter getting rich off the sweat and pain of the boxer. In the case of Moss, the relationship evolved into a relationship of equals. Soose absorbed the punishment in the ring, but Moss ensured the financial survival for Billy Soose in his later years, outside the ring.

World War II cut Soose's career short. In 1942, Soose began his push for the light heavyweight championship after a brief reign over a portion of the Middleweight crown. His country called and Soose willingly volunteered for Naval duty. After the war, Soose's financial successes afforded him options denied to most other boxers. He no longer had to fight for survival, and when he was offered $100,000 for a major event, Soose, without hesitation, turned it down. He decided to go on with the rest of his life, and a great career in the ring was cut short. Soose would become a successful businessman and retire with grace. At the young age of 26, his boxing career was over but his life outside the ropes was just beginning.

Gene Sebastian was never to obtain the success his older brother exhibited in the ring, but was, in his own right, just as successful outside the ring. Sebastian attempted to follow his big brother's success in the ring but sadly did not have his brother's skill, or for that matter, his brother's support. Billy Soose viewed boxing as a very rough endeavor and discouraged Gene Sebastian from following in his footsteps.

Sebastian would instead go on to have a successful career in law enforcement and that included being one of the original thirty six Federal Air Marshals for the FAA. Gene spent a good portion of his adult life being on the front line in the war on terror, long before it was identified as such. In the late 60's, Sebastian became an authority on skyjackings and other terrorist activities. In the 1990's, he would make presentations warning Americans about the upcoming danger that would culminate in the 9/11 attacks on the World Trade Center. By the time 9/11 happened, Gene Sebastian was retired, but he understood full well, long before many others, the coming war clouds that were threatening the United States.

Sebastian, although long retired from active competition, continued to be involved in boxing as a referee and official in the State of Georgia, with one of his last acts devoted to keeping a promise to his brother, the difficult effort to get Billy inducted into the International Boxing Hall of Fame. With the aid of his son Scott, Gene Sebastian has been busy making the case for his brother.

This book reviews the career of Billy Soose, but is much more than that. The goal of the writers is to remind the readers of a bygone era of boxing. For most readers, the names of many boxers are not going to be familiar, yet you will be reading about some of boxing's greats, at a transitional time in the history of our sport. Many of these top notch boxers may have become lost in the pages of boxing history, but their ring accomplishments certainly merit our close scrutiny.

Billy Soose was far more than a boxer and Gene Sebastian was far more than just a loyal brother. Both men were part of a great generation that helped America win a war and establish the peace and prosperity that followed. Theyse two brothers were part of that memorable generation. This is their story.

The Story of Billy Soose

CHAPTER ONE:

In the Beginning

William Stephen Soose was born in Farrell, PA on August 2, 1915, to Hungarian immigrant John Soose and his native Pittsburgh wife, Mary Koran. The couple had been married for two years before older brother Jack was born, with his sister Marie following less than a year later. (Marie Soose was known to many of her close friends as Mary, and her oldest daughter was also named Marie.) Billy Soose was born two years later. Within a year, Mary Soose would be a widow, as John Soose succumbed to tuberculosis, not at all uncommon at the time. His death left Mary to raise three small children all alone. Billy Soose was not yet two, and would never have any memory of his biological father.

For John Soose, his journey to America was in search of a better way of life that he would never live to see, and it would be up to his sons to pursue those dreams. Often for many immigrants, it is the children who in the end succeed in following through on the dreams of their parents. John had come to the United States in search of a better way of life, but it was John's sons that would find the American dream.

Mary met Albert Sebastian at a Hungarian picnic dance in the summer of 1917, and they wed a year later. Albert was born in Olcztelke, Hungary in 1884 and served proudly in their army. Like so many others, he came to America from Budapest, via Ellis Island, with his uncle in 1913, at 19 years of age. At that time most of the Hungarian immigrants settled in the coal mining and steel mill areas of Northern West Virginia, Ohio and Western Pennsylvania. Both Albert Sebastian and John Soose were two examples of the Hungarian influx in this region. The young couple had two offspring, Renee, born in 1919, and Gene born in 1927.

Albert inherited three children from Mary's first marriage, with the newly married couple adding two more children to the family, one of whom was Gene. Albert raised Jack, Marie and Billy as his own. He would never formally adopt the three older children due to a lack of money, but considered them to be his own flesh and blood. As the Great Depression began, the Sebastian's had five children living under one roof, and Grandmother Koran as well. Albert, like many other Hungarian immigrants, worked in the steel mills as a heater, firing up the furnaces in the making of steel, with money proving a scarce commodity in the depression years.

The Soose/Sebastian family lived in a 'company house', in Farrell, rented by the employees. The house had a dirt basement and an attic. (Many companies would provide this type of housing for their employees, often as part of the salary package.) As the Great Depression wore on, Albert and Marie struggled to make ends meet. Like most Americans, they were poor, but as Peter Heller wrote in the April 1973 edition of

5

Boxing Illustrated: "His family was poor, but not destitute, and Billy recalled when I visited with him that his childhood was generally happy, with his mother seeing to it that the family, no matter what, had an annual vacation at the lake, even if Billy and the rest of the family did have to wind up working at the resort area to pay for their stay." To supplement their income, Mary took a job as a retail clerk in a department store.

During the early depression years Jack Soose joined the United States Air Corps where he would spend the next 28 years. Jack would be the first child to leave home, and this helped relieve the pressure on the family finances, as there was one less mouth to feed. (Jack would have four children of his own before passing away in 1989 of heart failure. Jack and Bill's sister both died of pneumonia at the age of 28, just as World War II had begun.)

Renee married Charles Kovacs in 1938 and left the Sebastian home. They would have no children, and Renee passed away in 2002, of natural causes. By the end of the 1930s, the family was able to move to a better home and location in Farrell, PA. The older siblings took on the task of taking care of Gene, the youngest.

CHAPTER TWO:

Fighting as an Amateur

Billy was just 15 when he began his amateur career as a 100 pounder. Billy, who was always followed by his younger brother, Gene, would go to an abandoned school building to work with his trainer Pinky Roth and about eight other youngsters. These young lads wanted to make a name for themselves as well as a good living for their families, and boxing was that one avenue they would pursue. Roth took immediate notice of the many fistic gifts that Billy was bestowed with.

At first Billy had to box under the name of Billy Walker, not wanting his mother to find out, for his mother did not approve of his boxing career. His stepfather worked valiantly to convince Mary that boxing would be good for Billy Soose. Mary's fears of something bad happening in the would ring never leave her, and as a result of those fears, she never saw Billy fight in the ring.

Boxing scribe Joseph X. Flannery wrote: "Billy was born in Farrell, near Pittsburgh. Young toughs would often beat Bill and his friends when they tried to use a bridge to get to school. One day he heard the sounds of bags being punched in an old abandoned schoolhouse. It was a gymnasium of sorts and he went in. Told that he was too young to practice there, he offered to do chores. Shortly after he was given the job, he was spending more time punching the bags than doing his chores." Muhammad Ali began his career in boxing when he walked into a gym looking for help in developing boxing skills; so he could punish those individuals who stole his bike. Billy Soose's motives also began with the need for self-defense.

Gene Sebastian would stand behind his older brother, as 'the little ring boy'. His job was to pump water from a nearby well into wooden buckets, and bring it into the washroom, where the fighters would use it to shower. (Billy Soose was close to his baby brother, Gene. Gene recalled fondly that when he was seven years old, Billy cried from worry when Gene was taken to the hospital to have his tonsils removed.)

Flannery continues: "At 15, Billy began fighting on weekends, collecting a tin watch as the 'prize.' Secretly, the sponsors would later pay him $2 for the return of the watch." This way, Soose maintained his amateur status while picking up some much needed cash. Billy Soose won matches and all the Golden Gloves Championships that he entered, from the 112 lb. class, all the way up to the 160 lb. class.

Boxing writer Wally Wachter wrote: "The young Soose was an unlikely candidate for a world championship, when as a thin, lanky teen-ager he did odd jobs around the Henry Routh A.C. boxing stable, located in the alleyway off Wallis Ave. in Farrell. His keen interest and dedication to the sport being apparent, and under Routh's supervision, he worked his way into the Farrell

Boosters Club weekly shows in Farrell. He became a crowd favorite."

Soose told writer Bruce Buschel, "Back in those days (around 1932) – they were Depression days really – we had a lot of white fighters because they couldn't find a job and could make some money climbing in the ring. Now with jobs as plentiful as they are, not many white boys are gonna get their heads knocked off for the money. I mean, to get into the boxing game all you need is a license, a pair of shoes and a pair of trunks, that's it. Only your poorest of people are gonna do it." Boxing is a sport that historically attracted those at the lower end of the socio- economic scale, and with the Great Depression, in the early 30's, many white youths would join with the minorities on the unemployment lines. For many of them, boxing was a way out of the poverty that was quickly spreading throughout the country.

By the time, Soose graduated from Farrell High School, he had won over 100 amateur fights with just two blemishes on his record. Sixty percent of his victories came via the knockout route and he had won numerous Golden Gloves titles. Brother Gene followed Billy and the entire amateur team to various amateur events, in the small towns surrounding Western Pennsylvania, as a spectator. Gene was now hooked and having his own dreams of prizefighting because of the large amount of time he spent with his brother and the other members of the team.

Joseph Flannery wrote, "Billy's reputation as a high school fighter caused many invitations from colleges. Paul Moss, a native of Farrell who became a scriptwriter in Hollywood, took an interest in Billy, got him a scholarship to Penn State, and became his manager. Billy accepted the scholarship only if Moss would get back to him the $10 that his mother paid to enroll him at the University of Pittsburgh. Moss got the refund and Billy went to Penn State".

On the other hand, Gene readily recalled an incident that showed yet another side of his brother. Gene said, "Bill tried to discourage me from boxing. He would always try to find some tough, bigger kids who were watching us train to box me. One of them gave me a good beating. I cried and cried. Billy got angry and wouldn't let me walk home with him. That was the last time I cried, even when I was hurt".

Interestingly enough, many in the local press, and the fight mob rooted against Billy. Rarely did Billy lose as an Amateur. One day, Albert Sebastian walked into a poolroom and overheard some fighters discussing upcoming matches. They didn't recognize Soose's father. He listened as the two men discussed Billy and how they would have to go to Chicago to find someone who could beat Soose. Sebastian challenged the two men's contempt of the local hero, and of course, his son.

Wally Wachter, Sports Editor of the local paper covered the boxing beat in those days. Here, in part, is what he wrote: "The sport of boxing was healthy in those days. The old Farrell Booster Club fight cards were automatic Tuesday night date cards for many in the area. Fans were as ardent in attending as they are today about not missing an episode of their favorite sit-com."

Wachter recalled that Billy Soose was a popular local favorite even as a gangly kid of scarcely 100 pounds. Part of Soose's appeal was the wholesome kid next-door aura. His parents, Albert and Mary, installed a fine sense of values in their offspring.

Soose, sometime after he had retired, told Buschel, "I was on the (smoker/bootleg) circuit for seven years (1931-1938). I fought over 175 fights (lost maybe six - no records were kept). In those days I was much too young to turn professional and I wanted to mature. I had to grow up first. Were they really amateur fights? Well, yes and no. You got paid either a robe or a few watches and, of course, traveling expenses. Maybe ten or fifteen bucks, which was not bad in the depression days. If you were fighting main bouts, you got a hundred and twenty five dollars". In the 30's, there was a fine line between amateur and professional status. Amateur programs were essentially preparation for the Professional ranks".

Soose's college boxing successes forced him to drop out of college since no one wanted to fight him. In 1937, Soose won the NCAA middleweight championship. The following year, the NCAA changed its rules to exclude fighters from fighting in the NCAA if they had won a Golden Gloves title. Soose lost his scholarship to Penn State and was forced to drop out of school. The 30's were tough economic times for the Sebastian family, and Soose did not have the resources to continue on his own.

Many writers and fans considered Billy Soose as perhaps the best collegiate boxer of all time. Sportswriter Johnny Pepe wrote,"Soose, before turning professional, was a student at Penn State, interested in becoming first, a doctor, then a lawyer, and after his interest in physical education heightened, as an instructor. Billy was probably the biggest amateur name ever in the Western Pennsylvania-Northeastern Ohio area, and was a welcome addition to any and all fight cards. He often drew upwards of 3,000 people to watch him fight at Farrell, and also appeared in Pittsburgh, Erie, Oil City, Franklin, Warren and Youngstown Ohio."

Of his college days, Soose stated, "When they changed the rules to get me out (of college), I had some nationwide publicity. I figured I knew enough about managing and fighting that I needed a publicity agent more then a professional manager."

In 1977, Billy Soose gave the following advice to Penn State light heavyweight champion and football player Jim Restauri, "Stay away from football. It's not good for you. They'll get at your knees". To which one of the authors can only add 'amen'. (Rusty Rubin suffered a knee damage from playing football.)

Of his college days, Soose reminisced, "Sixteen fights, sixteen kayos. Actually, I had already matriculated at the University of Pittsburgh when my old manager, Paul Moss, bless his soul – he's dead now – brought me to Penn State. I just fell in love with the campus and decided to come here. I didn't really work much with Leo Houck, the coach, because I had fought a lot before I got to Penn State. I had at least a hundred fights".

Joseph X. Flannery addressed this when he wrote: "Billy became a feared fighter. He won sixteen college matches and other schools began to scheme to get rid of him. A collegiate rule was adopted that anyone who had fought in Golden Gloves competition could not fight in college. While the rule applied to everyone, Billy got national publicity because it was clear it was made to get rid of him."

CHAPTER THREE:

Soose Goes Pro

After his second semester at Penn State, in 1938, Billy told his family that he had decided to turn professional. Soose headed to the West Coast and began his career under the management of movie star Dick Powell and his now good friend and Hollywood screenwriter Paul Moss. Gene recalled, "He told us he would be gone for about seven months." Soose added, "If you had any science to your boxing at all, you'd get picked. A trainer could get ten percent and some managers got a third. I'm one of the few guys that never got cut up that way. I never wanted a manager. That's where Paul Moss came in, a scenario writer in Hollywood. And Dick Powell, the actor, became my co-manager."

The late Paul Moss recalled, "When Billy Soose, after many years of amateur boxing decided to leave college and take a whirl at the professional boxing game, he went to Farrell, his hometown, and asked me to advise him. I knew nothing about the professional game." Moss figured that by going to Hollywood and the Pacific Coast, he could avoid working with the traditional but corrupt boxing managers and promoters.

Moss also recalled, "One day during this period Joan Blondell and husband Dick Powell were staying in Cleveland for a few days and they called me up and asked to visit with me." During this particular visit Paul happened to mention his new venture. Dick kidded him about it, and at that time he thought the idea only was a pretty good joke. When Paul and Billy went to Hollywood, they soon became welcome visitors in the Powell home. Paul thought this was a lucky break for Billy, for he says the Powell home was unusually wholesome and worthwhile. Soose went to Hollywood at the beginning of his boxing career. While in California, there is little doubt that he entertained a professional acting career as well.

For Billy's debut into Pacific Coast boxing, Paul was able to match him with an ex-Marine pugilist in a preliminary bout on a program of fights in Hollywood, in which the great champion Henry Armstrong fought Baby Arizmendi in the main bout. All Hollywood was on hand, with movie greats and near-greats in ringside seats. Billy's appearance in the ring initially brought an expression of groans and protests from the ringside spectators. He looked youthful and smallish when compared with the stocky opponent, hard-faced ex-marine, Johnny Dean, in the opposite corner. 'He'll be killed!' seemed to be the universal thought and comment.

In the first round Billy started cautiously at first, though he managed to floor his man just as the bell rang to end the round. In the forth round Soose scored a knockout. Paul Moss said that he would never forget the instantaneous roar of applause from the once doubting crowd. Billy had quickly conquered Hollywood and made believers of the fans. After that fight, Dick Powell 'took a piece of him' as the saying goes.

Moss remembers that Soose had a constant interest in developing his mind as well as his personality. His goal was to finish his college education and prepare for a career after boxing.

Sports writer Joseph X. Flannery wrote, "Moss took Bill to Hollywood where he met actor Dick Powell, who became his co-manager for 18 months. He fought and won fights in Hollywood. During his leisure time, he was tested for several screen parts, but his boxing career prospered".

Wally Wachter later wrote before Soose's 1994 induction into the Los Angeles based World Boxing Hall of Fame: "Billy's career followed a scenario something like one his manager, Paul Moss, a Hollywood film writer, would have done for the screen. It had its snags along the way, but none reflected on Billy's ability. Matter of fact, the first case came when his college scholarship was ended in his junior year at Penn State University because he was 'too good. The second (setback) came with a hand injury in his eighth pro fight which threatened his career." This injury actually would affect Soose's career.

Moss, like Billy, was a Farrell native. Moss's family had a long established furniture business in town. After his graduation from Penn State, Paul went to Hollywood to work as a screenwriter, and established many strong contacts with movie stars, producers and moguls.

Wacther continued on Soose's relationship with Moss: "With prodding from his manager-to-be Moss, he accepted the Penn State scholarship. He was hailed as the greatest college boxer of all-time, within two years he had won all of his 16 bouts, all by knockouts. His knockout power was so feared that by his junior year two Universities threatened not to compete against Penn State if Soose remained on the team. The Eastern Intercollegiate Athletic Association (EIAA), in 1938, banned all Golden Gloves boxing champions from collegiate competition". This was a decision aimed expressly at Billy.

Billy Soose left Farrell, PA. for Hollywood, to live with Powell and his wife, actress Joan Blondell for seven months. Billy Soose, under the guidance of Paul Moss, made his professional boxing debut in LA on March15, 1938. He then won his next four bouts in California as well, three by knockout.

Wachter wrote: "That Moss followed Soose's amateur career with interest, and with Billy's decision to turn pro, agreed to become his manager. He solicited the support of the late move actor-singer Dick Powell on Billy's behalf. Powell, and his first wife, the late Joan Blondell, came to see Billy launch his pro career." Soose disposed of his first opponent, Johnny Dean, with a kayo victory. The victory was unexpected by many in the crowd, but afterwards, Soose won the crowd over.

Soose continued on his winning streak, and in his fifth fight defeated Johnny Foster, a tough, veteran pugilist with 28 wins against 24 losses. Billy Soose out-pointed Foster in easy fashion and was now ready to make a triumphant return to Pittsburgh.

So, Billy and co-manager Paul Moss departed California to return home in the summer of 1938

(July 25th) to fight his first 10-round bout against Al Quail, a tough, veteran brawler from Pittsburgh. This was the fight that was to change Billy Soose from being a big puncher and dictate the needed change to outstanding boxer.

Joseph X. Flannery writes: "He got a $1,000 offer to fight in Pittsburgh; a huge sum for a beginner. He checked to see if it was legitimate. The promoter misread the inquiry and upped the purse to $1,500."

Quail came into this fight with 32 wins against only 11 defeats and a draw. For Soose, this represented another step up and a match with someone who proved to be his toughest opponent. The inexperienced and undefeated fighter received his first boxing education as he hit the canvas in the third round from a Quail hook. Soose appeared shaken, but was not hurt as he smartly waited until the nine count before rising. In the fourth, he floored Quail after being stunned by a Quail right.

In the fifth round, Soose nailed Quail with a combination of rights and lefts, but the veteran

Quail was able to use all of his ring smarts to survive. Soose took control of the fight from this point and went on to score an easy decision.

Although Soose won the 10-round decision, he suffered very serious damage to his right hand. When he floored Quail in the fourth round with a big right, he permanently damaged all the tissues behind his right middle knuckle. Soose suffered a separation of the ligaments between the middle and ring fingers on his right hand. Despite surgery and months of layoff, the right hand never recovered. From this point, Soose would become a boxer and his days as a power puncher ended.

Years later, Soose would always say to media and fans alike: "I could only throw one good right in my future fights. After that the hand would blow up like a balloon. I always had to have a bucket of ice water after the fights to keep the swelling down."

Billy had to learn to stick and move (jab and back-off), and to double up on his jab in an instant, and the now single-fisted middleweight had to adopt to a brand new style, and quickly.

He seldom would use his right hand in his future bouts, as the hand would always swell so badly. His brother Gene noted, "You couldn't see the knuckles in his hand, they were usually swollen as far back as the wrist bone."

Billy suffered a lot of pain. He underwent several operations and therapy, but to no avail. His Sunday punch, the big right hand with the one punch kayo power, was gone.

From this point, Soose abandoned all thoughts of brawling and slugging and utilized his jab to keep the action at long range. His left jabs and clever legwork had boxing pundits reminding them of the classic style of 'Gentleman' Jim Corbett.

Finally Manager Paul Moss and Actor Dick Powell raised the necessary money for a second operation, this time from one of the top orthopedic surgeons in the country, which helped for a short time, but in truth, would never come close to solving the problem.

Besides his victory over Al Quail, a one-handed Soose had six more fights in 1938, knocking out former champ "Babe" Risko in three rounds on October 5,1938. He stopped clever boxer-puncher Eric Lawson in six rounds. The Eric Lawson fight would make the press and public sit up and take notice of what a fine boxer Billy had now become, and how smoothly he was able to make the transition from puncher. Billy became a smart fighter who knew how to make his one-good hand, his left, operate as smoothly as a well-oiled piston in an auto engine.

Wally Wachter writes: "Not allowing the injured hand to stand in his way, Soose returned to boxing and continued to move with ease through the ranks of middleweight contenders."

It was on a scouting session for a training site that Billy and Moss found Lake Wallenpaupak (in the Pocono Mountains). Moss and Soose then purchased 300 acres of wooded shoreline. Soose would set up an outdoor ring where spectators watched as the would-be champion prepared for his next bout. This piece of real estate would be the foundation of Soose's post boxing career. Here, he regularly entertained famous actors, politicians and sports writers. Soose eventually would buy out Moss's part of the investment and still later added additional acreage to develop the resort.

Billy's first loss was to Johnny Duca, who won a decision over the young Pennsylvania native in Lancaster, Pa. Soose would revenge this loss three months later in Youngstown, Ohio, as he took a decision from Duca. Paul Moss would then sign a contract for Billy to fight Charlie Burley. When told of the proposed fight, Ray Arcel, legendary manager and now Soose's trainer wondered out loud, "Why are you doing this?" Billy's right hand was not yet completely healed, and Arcel feared that without the use of his right hand, Soose had no chance to win. Many questioned the wisdom of fighting Burley, but money was always an important motivator.

Ray Arcel told Ring's magazine Roger Mooney, "I looked at him (Moss) and thought he was crazy. Nobody would fight Charley Burley. He was outstanding. He was the uncrowned middleweight champion. Heavyweights would not fight him, that's how great he was!" Arcel added that not even the great Sugar Ray Robinson would fight Burley adding that Burley "had to fight heavyweights in order to make a few bucks. The guy was a master." Burley, like Soose, was a Pittsburgh native though his race handicapped his boxing career. Soose had defeated Burley in the amateurs but Burley was one fighter that no one wanted to tangle with. He made all his opponents look bad.

On Nov.22, 1938, Billy fought a ten round decision against the great Charley Burley, in Pittsburgh. Arcel knew that Soose would be in a struggle and warned Soose that Burley, "In this guy mind, you are nothing." Arcel told his charge that nobody would expect the underdog Soose to win and advised, "You are on the defense, just move and box like you're shadow boxing." Arcel's goal was to have Soose fight from a distance and take advantage of any mistakes that Burley would make.

Soose came into the fight weighing 156 pounds, with Burley weighing152 pounds. Reporter Regis Welsh viewed this as a test between two up and coming fighters, and felt that Soose would challenge Burley. Welsh stated, "There seems little doubt that Burley is the best fighter of his pounds developed here in recent years. A natural welterweight (he) is building himself up beyond 150 pounds…. Soose, who is still developing, has not yet reached the stature of a full-fledge middleweight."

Burley started fast and bullied Soose. Soose ended the round with a solid right hand but it did little to deter Burley. In the second round, Burley attacked Soose with hooks to the body and some accurate rights to the head. Soose appeared in danger of being stopped." Soose survived even though Burley crowded Soose and wouldn't allow Soose to unleash his left jab or extend any of his punches. Soose got back in the fight in the fourth round, much to the surprise and dismay of Burley.

Between the fifth and ninth rounds, Burley pressured Soose with his craftsmanship and left jab. His right hand began to find Soose with regularity. As the fight progressed, Soose strengthened his resolve and became stronger.

Welsh observed, "Soose won admiration from the crowd by surviving three terrific opening rounds to come thundering into the homestretch like a thoroughbred showing his best at the finish." Welsh added that Soose's, "bad hands, his shortcoming since he began bouncing them off the more rugged chins of fellows like Burley, again bothered Soose."

Soose took the fight to Burley in the ninth. He nailed Burley with a big left hook and connected on a couple of solid rights. Burley would hold his ground but it set up the tenth and final phase of the fight. Burley chose not to rest on his laurels, refusing to take a decision for granted. Soose and Burley traded punches. Burley's experience allowed him to roll with Soose's punches, but Soose connected enough to win the round. Welsh commented, "Soose, disdaining things which had troubled him earlier, looked like the fighter he should be." Soose's comeback in the tenth did not change the result as Burley had built up such an early lead.

During much of the fight, Burley held the edge in the contest. The official score had 5 rounds in Burley's favor, whereas Soose was given credit for three rounds with two even. As Gene Sebastian told me, "This fight could have gone either way with two rounds even. It could have ended in a draw or this could have gone seven rounds to three in Burley's favor."

After that fight Billy returned to the dressing room with tears in his eyes. Ray Arcel said, "What the hell are you crying about? You just lost a split decision to one of the greatest fighters in the world; a fighter nobody wants to fight and you fought him with one hand. What if you had two good hands?"

Before the fight, Paul Moss said, "I'm not sleeping nights because everybody tells me that my fighter will get knocked out." Another legendary trainer, Eddie Futch once stated that Burley was the best pound for pound fighter that he had ever seen, even better then the great Sugar Ray Robinson. In his only professional fight with Burley, Soose was hampered by the damaged hand, and lost a close but fair decision. Burley was one of the great fighters who never fought for a title, and Burley came into this fight with more victories (21-2) than Soose had fights. Soose took a chance that not even Sugar Ray would take, and while he lost the fight he gained respect.

Unlike the fighters of today who seem to be content fighting three or four times a year, Billy Soose fought eight times from Feb. 20th, to Dec. 13th, 1939, losing only to Georgie Abrams via a 10 round decision on December 25, 1939, in Pittsburgh. Abrams was the one fighter who seemed to have Soose's number; beating Soose all three times they fought. In their first fight, Abrams rallied after being in trouble in the first and the fifth rounds. Billy's boxing skills allowed him to persevere and this set a pattern in their trilogy. In the Soose era, this boxing schedule was not at all unusual. Archie Moore and Sugar Ray Robinson finished with over 200 fights in their careers. Among notable fights in the 1939 campaign, was Billy's victory over Paul Pirrone, a veteran of over 100 fights with 88-recorded victories.

Soose was now getting close to a middleweight championship. In 1939 and 1940, the New York State Athletic Commission and the National Boxing Association would recognize separate champions in separate weight divisions, including the middleweight class. The sport of boxing has always been plagued throughout its history with various governing bodies competing against one another.

Ken Overlin, managed by Chris Dundee (brother of the legendary trainer Angelo Dundee), was the New York State Athletic Commission middleweight champ with the NBA recognizing Al Hostack.

Billy Soose ended 1939 with a fifth round stoppage of Jimmy Jones in Baltimore, MD. Soose showed a stiff left jab that paralyzed Jones, and in the fourth round Soose nailed Jones with a huge right hand that stunned the outclassed opponent. In the fifth, Billy once again nailed Jones with a right hand, and the referee called a halt after 1:18. This was Soose's 10th knockout of his career. But Billy would only record three more stoppages in his career. Enhanced competition combined with his bad right hand had officially ended Billy Soose's career as a power puncher. Gene Sebastian told the authors that after every fight, Soose would have to soak his right hand in an ice bucket to help relieve the pain and swelling.

CHAPTER FOUR:

1940- Soose Joins the Elites

Billy Soose had one important thing going for him-his trainer, Ray Arcel. In the Scranton Tribune Sports section of Nov. 5,1988, Guy Valvano writes as part of a tribute to legendary trainer/cutman Ray Arcel: "Billy Soose, one of a record 20 world champions who benefited from the expertise of Ray Arcel, learned more than just the rudiments of boxing from the man known as the 'dean of American trainers."

Soose's boxing style and refined manner outside the ring proved a vivid contrast to the rugged fighters of the day, such as Ken Overlin as well as Tony Zale, a fighter raised in the steel mills of Gary, Indiana. For some boxing pundits, the slick boxing Soose did not provide the same excitement as the brawling style of his counterparts. Some fighters and fans scoffed at the college educated and refined Soose.

"The college boy never lived who could really fight," said light heavy weight great Billy Conn before his 1940 fight with New York University alumnus Bob Pastor. As if to prove his point, Conn scored a 13th round knockout in the fight. In the early 40's, brawn took a backseat to brains when it came to fighting. (Conn, himself, was a cute boxer whose style nearly won him the heavyweight title against Joe Louis. For twelve rounds, Conn's boxing style dominated Louis before he decided to go against his corner's advice and to trade punches with the more powerful Louis. Louis knocked Conn out in the thirteenth round.)

Billy Soose looked the part of Joe College all the way. At 6-foot, Soose had an intellectual air about him that stated that he should studying Einstein's theory of relativity as opposed to engaging in the art of one on one fistic endeavor. One writer wrote of Soose, "A seasoned pug could send him back to the books in no time, right? Wrong. Billy Soose was no egghead. He more than held his own with the toughest fighters in his division." And his boxing style, which was scientifically simple using a good defense mixed with straight, sharp punching. This was really the stuff of a college fighter. In a sport where brawn often took precedence over brains, Soose showed that intelligence could indeed conquer brawn.

Billy Soose began the 1940 campaign with three fights over a two-week period. He bested Vince Pimpinella with an easy eight round decision followed up with a three round knockout of Jimmy Clark. The trilogy closed with another decision, this time over Brockton, Massachusetts native Bud Mignault.

Georgie Abrams again came into Soose's backyard and continued his mastery over Soose, as he took another 10 round decision. If there was a mystery that Soose would never solve, it was the slick Jewish boxer from Washington D.C. In their second fight, Soose began fast, dropping Abrams twice with short left hooks on the chin. Abrams recovered from the first round and nailed Soose with short flurries. Billy lost the third round due to a point deduction due to a low blow, and lost the seventh as well because of the same infraction. Abrams knocked Soose down with a sharp right in the fourth. Soose uncorked his left jab in the sixth round and showed life down the stretch. He took the eighth round as well and would have taken the seventh, except for another point deduction. The ninth was even as both men traded jabs, but the final round was all Abrams. Abrams moved inside the Soose left jab and pounded the body to take the decision. Penalties and Abrams' boxing savvy wasted Soose's fast start. After the fight, reporter Harry Keck wrote, "Unlike Conn, who obviously liked to fight, Soose looked like someone for whom fighting is not the thing he'd rather do if he had the choice. By that I do not infer that he lacks gameness, but rather that he had no enthusiasm for this business."

Three weeks later, Soose knocked out Enzo Iannozzi to atone for his loss to Abrams. The furor began to mount for a Billy Soose challenge to the Middleweight championship. Billy Soose continued his winning ways as he defeated Frankie Nelson and veteran Eddie Pierce. Pierce had conquered 58 fighters in his 86 fights. (Pierce had 12 draws to go with his 58 victories.)

On May 30th, Billy Soose warmed up for his upcoming bout with Ken Overlin with an easy decision over Jackie Ennis. The referee for the fight was the former lightweight champion, Benny Leonard.

On July 24th, 1940, Billy Soose squared off with the reigning New York recognized champion, Ken Overlin in a non-title bout. Both fighters came into the fight over the 160- pound level. This was a common practice in those days for a champion to fight a leading contender, and yet not put his title on the line. New York Times reporter John Kieran observed, "Overlin and Zale, making arrangements for their meeting with Soose, retained enough presence of mind to stipulate for over the weight matches. It's an old boxing custom. In that way, a champion can get his ears scrambled without disturbing his crown. It may upset his dignity a bit and tarnish his prestige a trifle but the championship is safe and that's the main thing."

These over-the weight-limit matches allowed champions to take on the leading challengers without putting their title at risk, and in some cases, it built momentum toward a rematch for much bigger purses. It fit into a marketing ploy as well as protected the fighter's belt. (Billy Soose would do the exact same thing a year later when he again fought Abrams after wrestling the title away from Overlin.)

The first Overlin-Soose match was held in Scranton, PA. Overlin came into the bout undefeated over his past 19 fights and was the favorite. Overlin came on strong in the first two rounds using effective hooks to the body and head to offset Soose's height and reach advantage.

In the third round, Soose staggered Overlin with two straight right hands, thus dominating the round. The fourth round began as the third ended, with Soose delivering several hard shots over Overlin. Overlin fought back furiously from the middle of the round.

Overlin began to take some momentum back with effective hooking and continued his attack through the next two rounds. In the eighth, Soose once again took control of the fight as he pounded Overlin. Overlin weakened as Soose nailed the champion with left jabs followed by rights. Rain fell on the outside ring over the last few rounds. As one writer noted, "Most of the fans stood up and put their ringside seats over their heads and others protected themselves with wearing apparel. It was a scene reminiscent of the first Dempsey-Tunney encounter at Philadelphia."

The ninth round saw Billy Soose continue his domination. While many ringside observers felt that Overlin won, it was the unanimous view that if this fight had lasted for 15 rounds, the championship distance at the time, Soose would have stopped Overlin.

The outcome however was a split decision with judges Mike Bernstein and Roy Edwards scoring the fight for Soose and referee Jack Walton voting for Overlin. Soose's strong finish enhanced his already solid reputation, and while the fight was fairly close, Soose's victory propelled him into the elites of the Middleweights contenders.

Ken Overlin had a reputation for being a playboy and night owl, and for his first fight with Soose, he was not in top shape. Overlin pressed his advantage in the opening rounds, and as the late rounds progressed Overlin had a slight lead. Soose came back in the later rounds and AP Jack Cuddy wrote, ""Soose came on like a ball of fire in the closing rounds."

Tony Zale and Billy Soose were scheduled to meet August 21st in yet another non-title bout. Both fighters came in over the middleweight limit of 160 pounds. Zale had won his version of the title the previous month by knocking out Al Hostak in Seattle. Zale was a vicious body puncher with plenty of power and stamina.

When Billy Soose defeated Zale, he won eight of the ten rounds. Zale aggressively came after Soose, but Soose's reach and speed bothered Zale. Fighting in Zale's backyard in Chicago, Soose fought one of his best fights against a future Hall of Fame fighter. As the third round opened, it was obvious who was the better fighter. Zale rushed Soose and Soose sidestepped Zale while peppering him with jabs. When Zale cornered Soose, Soose's quicker hands nailed the slower Zale. Soose took the decision and became the unofficial Middleweight champion.

However his claim to that crown was invalidated because he was two pounds over the 160-pound limit, while Zale was one pound over. He was denied the undisputed championship. Of the Zale fight, Soose remarked, "Tony Zale was a great fighter, but he was my easiest opponent. He had a style I could beat any time." As for the aftermath, Bruce Buschel wrote: "Billy is, without a doubt, the best boxer around and everybody knows it. No one knew it better than Tony Zale. No rematch (for the title). In boxing history, Billy Soose's name is in parentheses." Soose never received a second fight with Zale for Zale's portion of the title.

After the Zale fight, many considered Soose the Uncrowned Middleweight champion of the World. In November, Soose defeated Pimpinella for the second time in a year. His final bout was against Jimmy Casino. This was an easy bout since Soose took about every round and had Casino nearly out in the last round. However, Soose again injured his right hand and there was some fear that it was broken. With some major fights on the horizon, a broken right hand could have derailed his chances for a Middleweight title shot. Soose had a contract with the undefeated Tami Mauriello in Madison Square Garden for a January bout. This match-up was briefly put in doubt, but fortunately the X-Rays showed no breakage.

But title or no, Ring Magazine without hesitation, named him the uncrowned middleweight champion. How could they not? Anyone recall any other fighter beating two world champions in twenty-seven days?

The New York Times considered Soose's accomplishment the second most surprising boxing event just behind Pittsburgh fighter Fritzie Zivic's upset of Henry Armstrong. Soose finished the year as one of the top three Middleweights in the world.

CHAPTER FIVE:

Soose Goes for the Title

In the world of boxing today, it would appear that there are enough sanctioning bodies for every fighter to be declared champion. However, the large number of boxing sanctioning bodies is not a new state of affairs. As 1965 began, there were two world heavyweight champions-Muhammad Ali and Ernie Terrell. It would not be until 1967 when Ali defeated Terrell, that Ali would actually be the undisputed world heavyweight champion. For nearly three years after he beat Sonny Liston, Ali was not recognized as the undisputed heavyweight champion, incredible as it may sound.

Throughout boxing history, there have been moments during which numerous champions competed for championship recognition. In the late 60's, Jimmy Ellis and Joe Frazier both held the world heavyweight title while Ali was stripped of his title because he refused to serve in the military for what he cited were religious reasons (Viet Nam). 'Smokin' Joe Frazier would claim the mantle of undeclared champion on February 20, 1970 when he stopped Jimmy Ellis.

During the next decade, Frazier, Ali and Foreman would be the recognized world champions, but when Ali lost to Leon Spinks, multiple champions became the vogue once again. Spinks opted for a rematch with Ali instead of fighting Ken Norton, and the WBA withheld its recognition from Spinks. Ali would win the rematch and then retire, but from this point forward, there were numerous recognized heavyweight champions with very few moments of just one world champion. Ali's retirement in 1978 allowed Larry Holmes to capture the recognized championship mantle, but by the time the 80's rolled around, the various sanctioning bodies again declared their own champions at each weight division.

Throughout boxing history, the more successful promoters became influential in the governance of the sport as well as becoming boxers' managers. These promoters such as Michael Jacobs and Tex Rickard in the first half of the 20th century, and Bob Arum and Don King today, have proven to be effective in bringing new audiences to boxing as well as provoking public interesting the sport. The trio of Jack Dempsey, Jack Kearns (Dempsey's manager) and promoter Tex Rickard, grossed 8.4 million dollars in only five fights between 1921 and 1927. Tex Rickard became the main man in United States boxing till his death in 1929.

In the first two decades of the 20th century, the *Police Gazette* recognized champions and acted out the role that Ring Magazine provides today - a neutral observer of the pugilistic scene. In the1920's, the New York State Athletic Commission and the National Boxing Association began to sponsor "title fights." (The NBA evolved into the World Boxing Association in 1962, and its main rival, the WBC would be formed the following year.) These two groups would soon become rivals, and as a result, recognized different champions at different weight division.

The Walker Law established the New York State Athletic Commission, which allowed boxing matches to become legal in the state. New York became the center of the boxing universe, and Madison Square Garden its Mecca. The New York State Athletic Commission impact followed on the success of boxing in New York. As long as New York remained the center of the boxing world, the New York State Athletic Commission would remain the most powerful state commission.

The National Boxing Association, formed in 1921, originally represented 15 states with this organization representing a threat to the New York State Athletic Commission and New York boxing in general. This rivalry would lead to multiple champions almost from the beginning, and New York steadfastly refused to participate within the NBA structure. New York and its boxing establishment did not want to share its revenue and its influence with any of the other states or boxing organizations.

The New York State Athletic Commission would maintain its influence until the 60's when boxing began to migrate away from New York, and the sport's crime ridden structure was exposed. Ring Magazine tried in those days to mediate any controversy dealing with champions just as it is attempting to do today. Ring editor Nat Fleischer issued a monthly ranking of contenders and awarded its own championship belt.

As the 1930's began, there were three sanctioning bodies: the NBA, New York State Athletic State Commission and the European-based International Boxing Union. This state of affairs existed because of NBA's attempt to break the NYSAC boxing monopoly on titles. Many outside of New York felt that NYSAC favored New York boxers over others and they also felt NYSAC had a xenophobic attitude toward foreign boxers.

The Middleweight division was but just one example of this confusion. Author Peter Walsh declared the 1930's and early 40s as the era of the Muddleweights. Among those who were declared Middleweight champion by the NBA were Gorilla

Jones, Marcel Thil, Fred Apostoli and Ceferino Garcia. The NYSAC champions included Ben Jeby, Lou Broulillard, Vince Dundee, Teddy Yarosz, Eddie Risko, Freddie Steele, Al Hostak and Sonny Krieger, Ken Overlin and Billy Soose.

As 1940 began, Ken Overlin was the NYSAC Middleweight title holder and the NBA recognized Al Hostak, who would be beaten by Tony Zale that following July.

Peter Walsh wrote, "The New York State Athletic Commission was a law unto itself in the 1930's. It ran boxing by dictate. Its sporting rulers had power out of all proportion to their geographic area of control." Many fine fighters were frozen out of championship contender bouts. Walsh added that many hoodlums and mobsters gained control of the sport at the demise of Prohibition as the mob looked for new revenues.

In 1940, Billy Soose would defeat both champions, Overlin and Zale, in non-title fights. During this period, fighters would fight one another without putting their title at risk. The main way this was accomplished was through "over the weight" contests. A champion would contract with his challenger a fight that would be over the championship weight so the fight could not be recognized as a championship bout. When Billy Soose fought both Ken Overlin and Tony Zale, the contracts specifically called for the combatants to fight above the 160-pound weight.

After Tony Zale won his title, Ken Overlin desperately wanted a unification bout, but personal rivalries between managers prevented this fight from happening. Zale's manager, Sam Pian hated New York promoter Michael Jacobs. When Soose grabbed the title from Overlin, he had no better luck in getting Zale in the ring for a title bout for the same reason. Jacobs and Pian would not work together, and Jacobs helped promote Soose as he had promoted Overlin. Soose would beat both fighters in 1940, but only Overlin would put his title at risk a year later. Soose would never have the opportunity to fight Zale for his share of the title.

Today's situation is just a continuation of past political battles over control. The history of the

Middleweights of the 1930's is comparable to what is happening today. While boxing fans long for the day of a single champion in each division, the reality is that today's muddled affairs are reflective of past boxing history. Throughout boxing history, multiple champions were always a part of the sport. This was the world of boxing facing Billy Soose as he prepared to take the title. He could not just win one title bout to be the undisputed champion, he had to win two bouts to claim that title.

The first big event in the Middleweight division was the Billy Soose-Tami Mauriello fight. Tami Mauriello was undefeated and a rising star. For Soose, a victory would bring him closer to a title bout with Ken Overlin. Soose was the favorite. For Mauriello, this was his debut as a main event at the Garden. For Soose, it was also his Garden debut. In the 1940's, the Garden was the Mecca of boxing and more often than not, the Garden staged the main events. The first Ali-Frazier fight was held at the Garden, demonstrating that even in the 70's, the Garden was still hallowed ground.

This was a battle between the boxer and a devastating puncher. The bout proved no contest as Soose dominated the match. Mauriello found no solution for Soose's foot speed and left jab. Soose continued his march toward the Middleweight championship.

In one of the undercard fights, Ernie Vigh fought Coley Welch and now, he signed with Soose for a match in the Garden. Vigh, also of Hungarian decent, was a tough slugger with 38 knockouts in his 41 wins. Considered one of the division's harder punchers, Vigh provided a serious obstacle to the Soose express. Soose came into the fight as a 2 to 1 favorite. Vigh trained for this fight as hard as he had ever trained for a fight before. Beat Soose and Vigh would then be in line for a title against either Zale or Overlin. For both fighters, the stakes were high.

Soose's foot speed proved to be the difference as he out-boxed the slugging Vigh. The bout was close in scoring points, but the first seven rounds were essentially Soose's, as Vigh decided to box with a boxer. In the eighth round and behind on points, Vigh had to attack. A vicious left hook from Vigh nailed Soose at the end of the round. Vigh continued to chase after Soose, nailing him with left hooks and rights to the jaw. Soose countered with ineffectual punches as the body shots slowed the quicker Soose. Vigh was the fresher of the two fighters and for many boxing pundits, this fight damaged Soose's reputation. A nearly 3 to 1 favorite at fight time, Soose found himself weakly defending himself at the end of the fight.

Instead of a title fight with Overlin, Soose found himself with an important rematch with Vigh. Soose trained at Lake Wallenpaupack for this big bout. Win and he will have his long sought after Middleweight title shot. Lose and it would be back to ground zero.

Vigh told reporters, "Next time I won't make the same mistake in boxing him. I 'll fight him and knock him out." Soose commented, "Vigh was stronger, hit quicker and sharper than I thought. I was jarred by his left hook." Soose viewed Vigh as another Zale, and he easily beat

Zale. Overconfidence nearly derailed Soose's road to the title.

The rematch did not resemble the first fight at all. Soose knocked Vigh down with a short sharp right to the face. Vigh threw a loping right to Soose with Soose countering. The edge Billy had over his opponent was sharp punching. The right hand that leveled tough Ernie Vigh in the first round was as dynamic a wallop as anybody watching this event had ever laid eyes on. It left the hardened Garden fight crowd, previously unaware of Soose's hitting powers in awe. While Soose had to become a boxer after his hand injuries, he began his career as a puncher. In this fight, Ernie got up from the canvas, and proved to be the perfect foil for Soose's bag of tricks. Vigh attacked in the second and third rounds, but a Soose left right combination in the fourth round turned the tide of the fight for the final time.

From this point, Soose's left jab peppered Vigh, and Vigh could never penetrate Soose's defenses. This victory ensured Soose a chance at Ken Overlin's title.

Promoter Michael Jacob wanted to match the winner with Tony Zale and unify the title.

That win forced Ken Overlin to fight Soose for the title, or vacate it. The fans and boxing pundits clamored for this fight. Soose earned his shot at a title and for this fight; the belt would finally be on the line. Billy Soose stepped into the ring on May 9, 1941, with Ken Overlin in Madison Square Garden in NYC. Overlin was confidant that he could avenge his loss, and felt he had won the previous fight. Managed by Chris Dundee, the brother of the legendary Angelo Dundee, Overlin prepared for this fight as he had no other.

About Overlin's mindset before the fight, reporter Bob Considine wrote, "It is our embarrassing duty to tell you that Ken Overlin... really hates Soose...or rather he hates Soose's manager Paul Moss. He thinks Paul, who seems to be a rather harmless sort of fellow to us, put something over on him in Scranton last summer when the judges awarded Soose the verdict in that much discussed non-title fight."

Overlin's only goal was to embarrass and knock Soose out. As one reporter wrote, "Ken's current ambition as of press time is to knock Soose into Moss's lap to prove if nothing else that Sam Goldwyn was right when he said that a rolling Moss gathers the Soose that laid the golden egg." Overlin, like Soose, was not a knock out artist but this night Overlin came to fight. He was ready to rumble. At this point in their careers, both men had nearly 400 professional and amateur fights.

The fight was a contrast to their first bout. In their first bout, Overlin tired in the stretch and was barely hanging on as the bell sounded. Soose outboxed Overlin and avoided most of Overlin's harder punches. For the title bout, Soose decided that to win the title, he must be aggressive. The old adage in boxing was that you have to take another guy's title.

Soose was the aggressor but Overlin's accuracy bothered Soose. Overlin answered Soose's jab with his own. Soose targeted Overlin's face with Overlin countering with hooks to the head and body. Throughout the fight, Overlin clinched to neutralize Soose's attack, with the extra wrestling designed to weaken the boxer.

The first round saw Overlin nailing Soose with solid body shots. In the second round, a boxing match ensued with both men showing fancy footwork and agility. By the third round, the pattern for the rest of the fight developed. Soose pursued and Overlin boxed. Overlin countered the aggressive Soose and then tied him up.

In the fourth round, Soose staggered Overlin with a sharp right, and in the seventh, both fighters went toe to toe. In the ninth round, Soose once again would stagger Overlin, and Overlin spent the rest of the bout boxing and escaping.

Soose pursued and Overlin boxed In the sixth round, fighter announcer Sam Taub noticed that Overlin was slowing down and Soose appeared to be the stronger of the two. At the end of the seventh, both men went toe to toe for a brief moment but for the most part, it was Overlin backed up into the rope as Soose pursued.

Overlin hooked to the body and head as Soose came forward. Overlin's counterpunching was scoring. In the ninth round, Soose landed a hard right and followed with a left to the body that had Overlin hanging on for dear life. In the tenth, Soose had Overlin in trouble one more time as he tried to finish off the champion. The eleventh was not much different as this fight appeared to follow the script of the first fight with Overlin tiring in the later rounds. In between rounds, the champion glanced briefly at the ringside reporters. Overlin rallied as he boxed and moved out of Soose's range. Both men boxed well though Overlin managed to avoid Soose's harder punches. As the final round opened, the now exhausted Overlin looked like he might go the distance as he grabbed Soose at every opportunity. He managed to survive, but Soose grabbed his championship belt.

In the eyes of many boxing pundits at ringside, Overlin may have gotten the better of Soose in the later rounds. The decision was close and most of the boxing fans watching the match felt that Overlin won. The Associated Press had Overlin winning 11 rounds to four. The judges rewarded Soose for his aggressiveness. Referee Arthur

Donovan and judge Marty Monroe gave Soose 8 rounds to 7 whereas Judge Bill Healy scored it 9-5-with one round even. Overlin's constant holding, and Soose's aggressiveness proved to be the difference.

After he won the title Ray Arcel told Billy "You won the title with one hand, with two you could beat the world!" Of the Overlin title fight, Peter Heller writes: "Billy remembers, 'I had beaten Zale and I had beaten Overlin. Chris Dundee (Overlin's manager) didn't want me to fight Overlin because he knew I'd beat him. He wanted to keep it (the title) as long as he could so he tried to get somebody else in a title bout. But finally the newspapers made him fight me. It wasn't really a tough fight, but it was a grueling fight. We were both cuties and he'd stick and I'd grab and I'd stick and he'd grab. It was a bad fight; really, it wasn't a good fight to watch. I wanted to win the title. I didn't care what it looked like." The Soose family returned home to Farrell and a hero's welcome, as Billy Soose had brought a bit of boxing history to the small Pennsylvania town.

Gene was only 14 years old when Billy won the title. Their father, Albert, and a few friends from Farrell, PA., made the eleven-hour drive to NYC to watch the fight. Billy and his dad cried with pride at Billy's victory. The photographers took pictures of the family in the dressing room after the fight. The following day they celebrated in NYC watching a Broadway show called *Hells a Poppin*. For Gene it was his first taste of a Broadway show. This fight merely whetted the appetite to follow in his brother's footsteps.

Soose's victory over Overlin was the high water mark in his boxing career. While Chris Dundee protested the decision, the New York boxing commission upheld the verdict. Soose was now one of the two world champions.

CHAPTER SIX:

Light Heavyweight Campaign and Navy Enlistment

In Soose's next fight he won an easy non-title bout against Tony Celli, knocking Celli out in the second round. Celli came in at 173 pounds, and Soose dominated the heavier Celli. In the second round, Soose scored several hard shots featuring his left jab. Celli hit the floor almost immediately as the bell rang to open the second round, and found the canvas four more times before the referee stopped the fight.

Georgie Abrams wanted another crack at Soose and his title. Abrams would fight Soose, but it was in a non-title bout. While there was talk of another Soose-Overlin bout, Soose signed to fight Abrams. By not putting his title at risk, he was still guaranteed another bout with Overlin. This fight was the opposite of the Overlin-Soose fight, as Abrams plodded forward and Soose boxed. While many at ringside felt that Soose won this fight, Abrams constant forward movement won the judges card.

Soose nailed Abrams over and over with his left jab, but Abrams continued to plod toward Soose. The machine gun like jab of Soose could not discourage Abrams.

In the seventh round, Abrams nearly knocked Billy Soose down with a right hand that slipped through Soose's guard. Abrams continued the attack in the eighth and ninth as his combinations overwhelmed Soose's jab. In the final stanza, both men went toe to toe. Georgie Abrams held a slight margin in the exciting exchanges.

In scoring fights, some judges give the edge to the aggressive fighter whereas other judges will favor the boxer. In this bout, judges gave the edge to the aggressive fighter just as the judges favored Soose's aggressiveness in his title bout with Overlin.

Billy Soose was scheduled to meet Ceferino Garcia for the title in Los Angeles. However, the California Boxing Commission aligned itself with the National Boxing Association, which recognized Tony Zale. So the fight became a 12 round non-title bout.

This fight proved to be as controversial as the Abrams bout. Soose dominated the fight with his jab. With the fight in control, Soose's head clashed with Garcia. An ugly gash opened up and the referee called it an accidental head butt. A wide gash opened up on Soose's left eye below the brow.

Garcia unleashed his bolo uppercut at the bloody eye. The gash opened up wider and the referee stopped the fight. The referee declared it a technical draw. (Today, Soose would have been awarded the victory since he had won five of the seven rounds fought. When a fight is stopped due to an accidental head butt, the bout goes to the scorecard provided that four full rounds have been completed. If the fight is stopped before the fourth round, then the bout is considered a technical draw.)

But Billy was having problems keeping his large, 6′1″ frame at the smaller weight level of 160 lbs., so on Nov. 18, 1941 Soose vacated the title and decided to campaign at light heavyweight. There was no super middleweight division in those days. In his first fight at 175 lbs., Billy trounced highly rated contender for the light heavyweight title, Jimmy Reeves.

Reeves came out fast as he landed several right hands. Soose's left jabs found their range as Soose started to take command of the fight. Starting in the third round, Soose out fought Reeves. Reeves hit the canvas, and the fight was essentially over when a Soose right hand found his jaw. The fight occurred twelve days after the Japanese attack of Pearl Harbor.

Soose was now the leading contender for Gus Lesnevich's light heavyweight title. Jimmy Bivins was his opponent. Soose came into the fight at 172 pounds and Bivins weighed 178 pounds. Bivins won most of the rounds dominating Soose.

"Bevins was a tough guy," Billy recalled of that 10-round match in Cleveland – his third as a light heavyweight. While Soose was nearly two inches taller, Bivins had long arms, and his jab kept Soose off balance. Gene Sebastian told me that his brother admitted his difficulty in penetrating Bivins defenses and dealing with his unexpected longer reach. In the third round, Soose threw a sharp right that stunned Bivins, but Bivins survived. Soose again injured his right hand after that punch, and fought the rest the fight as a one handed fighter. Bivins easily won the decision and Gene Sebastian recalled, "Bivins was a great fighter and there was no doubt who won this decision."

This brawl would be Soose's last professional fight. It was 1942, and the United States was embroiled in World War II. Billy, like many other athletes of the day, enlisted in the Navy, and Billy Soose fought his last pro fight. Gene Sebastian told us that if World War II had not intervened, Soose would have fought for the light heavyweight championship. "I am biased but I felt that Billy could have beaten Gus Lesnevich," Gene said. "Lesnevich had a style similar to Zale and Soose had an easy fight against Zale." He added that he also felt that his older brother could have beaten Billy Conn had they fought. There was a natural rivalry between the two fighters as Billy Conn felt that the college educated Soose could never be a championship fighter. There was a distance between these two great Pittsburgh fighters that never could be eased by private meetings.

Billy Soose hung up the gloves shortly thereafter. His final ring record read an impressive 34-6-1 and he was never stopped in any of his bouts. As an amateur and a pro, Billy fought a total of 265 fights, and avenged his losses in rematches with the exception of Georgie Abrams, whose club-style fighting gave Soose trouble.

It was early in World War II, (February 1942) which Billy enlisted in the U.S. Navy, and became one of the first of many big name boxers and other athletes to enlist in America's Armed Forces. As a Chief Petty Officer he joined former heavyweight champions Gene Tunney and Arthur Mercante

Sr. Billy served in Alaska for 2 ½ years, being discharged at war's end in 1945, as an Ensign. When Billy entered the service, he promised his wife that he'd never fight again. He kept that promise.

After the war, there was a cry to match up two of Pittsburgh's best fighters, Billy Soose and Billy Conn. When Billy was discharged from the service he was offered $100,000 (huge money in those days) to fight either Billy Conn or Joe Louis. But Soose was done, he had accomplished his goal and there was no longer the need or desire to compete. He had nothing left to prove.

CHAPTER SEVEN:

Paul Moss

Some Farrell businessmen, backing Soose, convinced Paul Moss to manage Soose's career. Moss worked in radio and publicity in Hollywood. Moss wired money to Soose and pulled a publicity coup when he convinced Actor Dick Powell that he was going to manage the young fighter.

Moss and Soose had a unique relationship. At the time, writer Bob Considine wrote, "Soose's relationship with his manager, Paul Moss, has created downright alarm in the beak-breaking business. It is revolutionary in that there is no master-servant aspect to it." From Pennsylvania, Moss was a rugged looking, quick-witted manager and rarely stayed in Soose's corner during a fight. He had trouble watching his client get hit.

Moss was able to get Soose a job in a steel plant in the hope of strengthening Soose's damaged right hand after Soose's injury during the Quail fight. Moss arranged for Ray Arcel to train the young boxer. He also attempted to get Michael Jacobs to promote Soose's future fights.

He wrote Jacobs, "It is not my intent to bore you with words about this boy's fighting ability. Such a description would have to be secondhand if it were to carry any weight, since my experience in the boxing game is limited to what I have gathered around the country during the last six months, the sum total of which has convinced me that I know little or nothing. So I must rely on boxing men like Harry Keck, Ray Arcel and Nate Lewis, and I trust they are at least partly correct when they say he is the most outstanding fighting prospect in the ring today."

Paul Moss was a screenwriter, not a boxing manager. Moss convinced Dick Powell to be Soose's sponsor. At first, Powell felt the whole matter of being involved with a boxer more humorous than serious, but Moss persevered.

Powell agreed to work with Moss and invited Soose to live with him for seven months. The deal was consummated after Soose's first fight. Powell joined Soose's team.

Moss understood that Billy Soose was interested in much more than boxing. Soose still wished to graduate from college, and included among his goals - leave the boxing game with a little money. While he was in Hollywood, Soose tested for several screen parts including the *Lou Gehrig Story*. Moss's Hollywood contacts were to give Soose other career options but it was boxing that made Soose.

Being a Farrell native, Moss shared Soose's Western Pennsylvania roots and this aided in their relationship. Soose and his one-time manager and friend Paul Moss purchased a 17-room farmhouse and barn, on 424 acres in the Pocono's where Bill trained for his major fights.

After the war ended, Paul Moss sold his portion of the land to Billy, and Soose who then had the camp converted into a resort, complete with a large motel, bar, restaurant, cottages adjacent to the lake front, and a large boat marina. Moss's management skills and friendship helped to ease Soose's retirement.

The relationship between Moss and Soose ended gradually. After Soose rejected Jacobs offer to fight Louis and Conn, his boxing career was over. Moss was no longer needed to manage his boxing career and when Moss sold his share of the Pocono property, their relationship eventually evaporated. Like a sand castle that washed away from the waves on a lonely beach, their relationship merely swept away into history as both men went in different directions. Moss returned to historical obscurity, while Soose concentrated on his businesses.

CHAPTER EIGHT:

After the War, and Retirement

Before entering the service Billy Soose met and fell in love with Peggy Unger, a very beautiful coed who was attending Smith College. The two married in early 1942.Unfortunately, the marriage didn't work out, and Peggy and Bill divorced in the early 1950's. They had two children, daughters Carol and Willa.

In 1953, Soose's marriage collapsed as Peggy sued for divorce. The Soose's fought over custody and Peggy won the right to take care of both of the children. She would eventually remarry two more times. As for Billy Soose, he never remarried.

Frank Graham Jr. in an article of the July 15,1963 edition of Sports Illustrated closed a feature story on Billy Soose this way: "Soose has kept pace with the growth of his beloved lake. Prosperous and healthy at 46, he is full of plans for himself and his land "and why not? It's less than a hundred miles from New York City." Billy Soose established friendships with powerful politicians including Pennsylvania's Governor William Scranton. Scranton had Presidential ambitions and even did a brief run at the Republican nomination in 1964 with a last gasp effort to derail the Goldwater candidacy.

When Billy Soose was elected to the World Boxing Hall of Fame in 1994, noted boxing journalist Joseph X. Flannery wrote on January 22, 1995: "While Billy Soose has not boxed professionally since Jan 13, 1942, preferring the tranquility of life at Lake Wallenpaupack, he is not forgotten by the World of boxing. "Billy, who is 79, fought with brains rather than brawn. And after he earned enough to sustain himself he walked away without scars, or regrets."

After his three years in the Navy during World War II, Soose completed all his goals in boxing and was moving forward to achieve brand new goals. Soose's motel-tavern was a financial success and he owned over 325 acres fronting Lake Wallenpaupack. The original purchase price was $17,000 and it would eventually realize more than ten fold its worth. Located within this complex was an old barn, which served as his gym before Billy would switch it over to a tavern. The resort included a restaurant that was rated four stars.

After the war, Soose returned back to his old training spot at Lake Wallenpaupack – which he had bought before the war with Paul Moss – and developed a resort compound. He would sell his resort piecemeal over the years for over $1.7 million. Soose's two daughters, and his granddaughter and grandson visited Lake Wallenpaupack over the years to see him.

As the years went by, Billy Soose's reputation grew in the Pittsburgh area. When inducted into the Pennsylvania Boxing Hall of Fame, Chic Feldman wrote in the April 14th edition of The Scrantonian: "That Soose, by the quality, cleanliness and sportsmanship he brought to boxing, has eminently earned his place in the

Hall of Fame, is agreed by fistic men everywhere. "We know he belongs on the pedestal with (Pete) Latzo, Tommy Loughran, Lew Tendler and the other greats," Hall of Fame President Joe Sweeney emphasized. "The vote proves there wasn't the slightest doubt in our minds."

Soose wanted to stay active in boxing and expressed an interest in being on the Pennsylvania Boxing Commission. "Maybe you think I'm crazy," he says, "but I want to be on the boxing commission in Pennsylvania. I still like the sport, and I'd like to see it get started again. Putting it back into the high schools and colleges would be the first step."

Sports writer Ralph Kremer wrote, "Billy Soose is more than just an ex-fighter and keen businessman, but a deep thinking individual, possessing a rich gift of human psychology nurtured by nearly a dozen years in the ring. His interest in youth is tremendous, especially in the amateur boxing programs sponsored in nearby Scranton."

Soose told Kremer, "In what other sport can a man be more of an individualist, than racing another man in the ring? "The ring teaches a boy or man many valuable lessons."

Soose related how boxing taught him, "The value and supreme power of patience. Any man, who angers in the ring, is a loser even before he starts. This holds true in all dealings in life. Patience is the strongest force of power anyone can possess."

Soose was never stopped in the 41 fights that he participated in and the only major rival that seemed to have his number was Georgie Abrams. Soose's boxing career only spanned five years but Sandy Koufax and Dizzy Dean made it into the Baseball Hall of Fame in Cooperstown, NY, with short careers reduced due to injuries.

Later in life, Soose carried over two hundred pounds in weight, but little of it was fat. There are some sports writers who believed that Soose may have grown into a heavyweight had he continued.

In his younger days, Billy Soose was boxing's version of Jack Armstrong. Bruce Buschel wrote,

"In his younger, glossier days Billy Soose bore a Hollywood resemblance to Jack Armstrong: Wavy Ronnie Reagan hair, James Cagney dancing eyes, Mickey Rooney pug nose, Wallace Beery puffed cheeks, John Barrymore chin and Delores del Rio smile. A sports writer wrote that he had 'the prettiest footwork since Fred Astaire." His body, well, the body was something else. Middleweights always had the greatest bodies. They got Paul Newman to Play Rocky Graziano, right? If John Garfield were Irish he'd make a wonderful Billy Soose."

While most fighters end up with nothing after their careers either due to theft by their manager or by spending it all, Soose maintained a comfortable living after boxing. Of this, Soose stated, "Paul Moss, my manager, had money of his own. However, he had a special checking account for all the expenses that occurred. I paid all the expenses, and Paul did not receive any money at all. Ray Arcel, my trainer, was receiving 10 percent of the purse, and he was paid out of our expense account."

CHAPTER NINE:

The Case for Soose in the International Boxing Hall of Fame

In the late 30's and early 40's represented the golden era of Pittsburgh boxing, eclipsing even the era of the great Harry Greb, one of boxing's greats during the 1920's. In a two-year period, Billy Conn, Sammy Angott, Fritzie Zivic, Jackie Wilson and a slick college educated boxer named Billy Soose all claimed World titles.

We came across a letter from a boxing fan that described his first meeting with Billy Soose at the age of 83. The fan wrote, "I got to schmooze with Billy Soose (He's 83) and he has all his faculties, which is several more than I have! Speaking with the 83 year old Soose reminds me of the 80-year-old man who told his pal that he was marrying an 18 year old. 'Great Scot!" sez the friend, "An 80 year old marrying an 18 year old. Why, don't you realize such a union could be fatal? The old man shrugged, 'Well, if she dies, she dies.'"

Billy Soose was like that. A college educated fighter in a sport where education was never required and looked at with suspicion, Soose scrapped tooth and nail all the way to the top of the middleweight division and was moving to the top of the light heavyweight division before World War II shortened his illustrious career.

While attending Penn State, he fought for the Penn State boxing team. But after 16 straight demolitions in college competition, other college teams would not compete with Penn State as long as Soose fought for them. So Soose went off to the professional ranks. Soose entered the professional ranks with a slugger reputation, and combined with a 6 feet plus frame, Soose towered over most of his opponent.

Early in his career, Soose fought Al Quail, and in the process of beating Quail, he split the tendon on his middle knuckle. From this point on, Soose lost the power to punish his opponent and switched from slugger to boxer. Rarely can a fighter change styles in the midst of a career, but the greatness of Soose showed an adaptability rare in most boxers. Could you imagine George Foreman having to turn himself into a boxer? Or Joe Frazier? You can now understand the magnitude of what Soose accomplished.

A fighter becoming a puncher is not that odd, but a puncher becoming a boxer is almost unheard of.

But boxers like Soose are not lacking in power or the ability to punish other fighters. Virgil Hill, a fighter similar in style to Soose, put lickings on other fighters. In Billy's second fight with Ernie Vigh, Soose dropped Vigh with the perfect right hand. After the fight, referee Jim Crowley said, "Vigh fought in a dazed condition for five rounds." While Soose could no longer knock you out, he could hurt you after a deadly combination of punches.

After this fight, Soose would decision Ken Overlin for the Middleweight title. Soose had quickly climbed his Mount Everest but his ring career would soon be over. After a couple of bouts at Middleweight, Soose vacated his title and campaigned as a light heavyweight though his campaign was short lived. After two victories, Soose lost to future Hall of Famer Jimmy Bivins, a great boxer of the 40's. Then he enlisted in the Navy, never to fight again.

Soose was one of those fighters that time has forgotten. Boxing writer Herb Goldman ranked Soose as the 21st greatest middleweight and his victims included the likes of Ken Overlin and Tony Zale. Boxing historian and writer Rusty Rubin believed that Soose belongs in the International Boxing Hall of Fame and has been leading the charge for Soose's admission. Persuaded by Rubin's argument, co-author Tom Donelson joined the crusade to have Soose added to the International Boxing Hall of Fame.

Soose suffered from two major obstacles, neither easy to overcome. The first is that he was considered a light puncher and most boxing fans are prejudiced against the slick boxer, preferring the one-punch knockout fighter and the action he provides.

Many fans seem to prefer the slugger and the knock out artist. Even when a boxer is glorified, it is because of an occasional knock out. Boxers like Jack Johnson, Sugar Ray Robinson or Muhammad Ali could turn a fight around with one punch and finish their opponent. After his knuckle injury, Soose's strength was not his knock out punch, but his newly developed slick boxing skills that had been will honed, but rarely used, in an extensive amateur career.

The second problem is that Billy Soose did not have a long ring career. He quit boxing at the age of 26 and when his duty to Uncle Sam was completed, he kept his promise to his wife, not return to boxing, no matter how much money was offered. After World War II, Soose was only 30, but unlike other boxers such as Billy Conn and Joe Louis, he walked away from the sport, having neither his money depleted or his brains scrambled.

Sadly, we never truly saw Billy Soose in his prime for very long. As Soose was growing into a light heavyweight and entering his prime, first the war and later his retirement cut his career short. Without World War II, and his promise to his wife, who knows what glory would have lay in store for Billy Soose?

Soose's greatest accomplishment was not winning the title, but simply to be able to reinvent himself after hand injuries limited his knock out power. Using his reach and height, he became a boxer who avoided punishment.

In retirement, Billy maintained his zest for life. When confronted with Plan A gone astray, Soose simple adopted and went for Plan B. Soose's greatest strength was flexibility, a trait rare among most fighters. Scott Sebastian, Soose's nephew, told Rusty Rubin, "When I was a kid, boxing was a scientific game, mind and body functioning as one." Soose, as a fighter, developed into a scientific fighter when he injured his hand and was one of sweet science's polished boxers in the late 30's and early 40's".

As for Billy Soose's place in boxing history, noted boxing historian Angelo Prospero said, "The great New York governor and presidential candidate Alfred E. Smith once stated, 'Let's look at the record'. All we have to do is take a gppd look at Billy Soose's record as both a boxing world champion and as a man to realize he belongs in the Canasatota NY based International Boxing Hall of Fame."

Prospero added, "Out of the many champions, he is the only one who seems to have been largely ignored. The reason why is a mystery, especially since many minor figures, fringe champions and nefarious types have been embraced in the hallowed halls of Canastota."

For many boxing fans, Billy Soose is invisible and virtually non-existent. If World War II had not intervened or if Soose would have shown any interest in returning to boxing after the war, we might have a completely different perspective about Soose. After the war, Soose walked away from boxing and became lost in the purgatory that is boxing history - just waiting to be reclaimed. It's those of us who appreciate the history of boxing that have the duty to restore his name.

Soose stops Vigh

Soose won't remain cornered for long

Youngstown 1949

Trooper Gene Sebastian

Bill, Sister Renee, Brother Jack, Gene

Brothers, Jack, Bill, and Gene

State Trooper Gene

Dad, Gene Sebastian with Son, Scott

F.B.I. Academy, Quantico, VA. 1/11/74, Gene Sebastian, first from left

Billy Soose

Gene Sebastian

The Sebastian's today

THE

KNOCKOUT

LOUIS AND
GODOY SET
FOR L.A.

HAVE A RAFT
OF LAUGHS
ON PAGE 4.

HOLLYWOOD
TO SEE
BILLY SOOSE

BUDDY SCOTT
SEEKS COAST
BOUT.

BILLY SOOSE

THE
UNCROWNED
MIDDLEWEIGHT
CHAMPION
OF THE
WORLD.

SOOSE LICKED
KEN OVERLIN
AND
TONY ZALE
RECENTLY.

SOOSE FIGHTS
JIMMY CASINO
AT
HOLLYWOOD,
FRIDAY
NITE.

THE
UNCROWNED
CHAMPION
IS MANAGED
BY
PAUL MOSS.

10¢

10¢

Vol. 14   December 14, 1940   No. 51

99

The Ring — June 1941

LOUIS-SIMON FIGHT PICTURES

25 Cents PDC JUNE 1941

The RING

SOOSE,
...anding Contender
...or Middleweight Honors

BAB... ...REVIEWED

THE KNOCKOUT

Garcia on
Edge for
Soose
—
Bybee Is
So. Calif.
Jinx

Ducats Going
Fast for
Gallery Show
—
Wilson May
Box Jenkins
in L.A.

IT'S A "NATURAL"

SOOSE VS. GARCIA

MONDAY NITE
SEPTEMBER
15TH

BILLY SOOSE
MIDDLEWEIGHT CHAMP

AND IN ADDITION THERE WILL BE THE GREATEST SUPPORTING CARD IN L.A. BOXING HISTORY!

CEFERINO GARCIA
OWNER OF THE PARALYZING "BOLO PUNCH"

Tom Gallery presents Calif.'s first 12 round bout to a decision at Gilmore Ball Park, Sept. 15th.

10¢   10¢

Vol. 15   September 13, 1941   No. 37

101

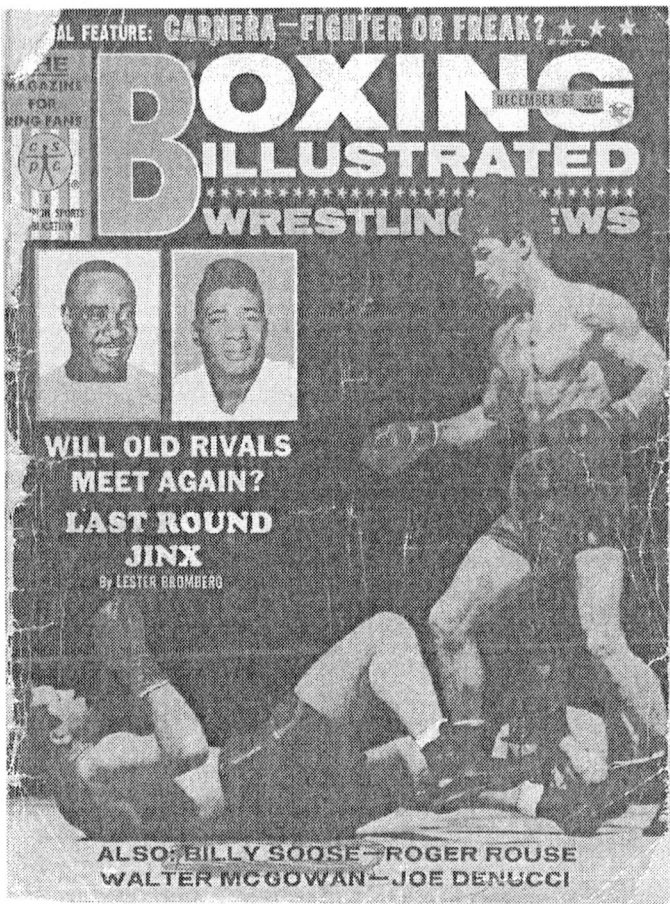

ROOMS · MODERN COTTAGES ·
LUXURIOUS EFFICIENCY MOTELS
LAND AVAILABLE IN EITHER
LOTS OR ACREAGE
DEEP WELL WATER SUPPLY AVAILABLE
LAND FOR LEASE

EXCELLENT CUSINE BAR
& COCKTAIL LOUNGE.
SNACK BAR · GIFT SHOP

BILLY SOOSE'S

"Comfortable Living in Healthful Surroundings"

IN THE POCONOS

LAKE WALLENPAUPACK :: TAFTON, PA.

TELEPHONE HAWLEY 3510

Your Host:
BILLY SOOSE
RETIRED MIDDLEWEIGHT CHAMPION
OF THE WORLD

February 19th, 1963

EDWARD S. MAUCHE?
GENERAL MANAGER

Mr. Hank Kaplan
6345 S. W. 4th St.
Miami 44, Florida

Dear Hank;

The Chairmanship for the Boxing Commission of our State will soon be selected, and I am one of the candidates for this position.

As you well know, boxing is in great need of new organization and thinking, throughout the country, and I am most eager to help restore it to the pinnacle it once so graciously held. I feel that with my own personal career as a fighter, and having had contacts with managers, promoters, and fighters, I would be better able to understand the problems that arise.

Because of your direct and active association with boxing, I feel that a personal letter of recommendation from you directly to Governor Bill Scranton, would be of the utmost importance. I will appreciate any consideration you may extend me.

My best personal regards to you and your continued success.

Sincerely,

Billy

Billy Soose

BS:j
Governor William Scranton
Office of the Governor
State Capitol
Harrisburg, Pennsylvania

P.S. Hope everything is ultra extra with you — and that you are enjoying good health —
Boxto Bill.

February 28, 1963

Governor William Scranton
Office of the Governor
State Capital
Harrisburg, Pa.

Dear Governor Scranton,

It is my understanding that your office is in the proccess of selecting a Chairman of the Pennsylvania Boxing Commission.

When this chairmanship comes to mind, the qualifications of one candidate, above all others, are immediately focused toward the requirements a leader of this nature should possess.

Billy Soose is this candidate. His formal and practical education make Mr. Soose admirably suited for this position. His many years of experience in physical education plus an extraordinary career in amateur and proffessional boxing, culminating in the highly respectable status of World Middleweight Champion, demonstrates his regard athletic achievement and physical fitness.

His demeanor and respectability while in boxing was of the highest plane. With his style of boxing he contributed a scientific approach to the sport which concentrated on skill, technique, ring tactics and brainy thinking as opposed to the concept of "brute Force" alone. His was a genuine contribution towards the betterment of boxing.

It is this improvement which Mr. Soose is capable of continuing today. The sport of boxing is in a dynamic state during this era and it is important that a leader of his qualifications be at the helm.

Mr. Soose has lived an exemplary life since retirement from boxing and is today, a successful and popular bussinessman.

In behalf of countless sports minded people throughout the United States, may I respectfully request that Mr. Billy Soose be given the opportunity to perpetuate the fine qualities of a sport which, historically, has always enjoyed much popularity in the State of Pennsylvania.

Very truly yours,

Hank Kaplan

(Form of Contract required by the Pennsylvania State Athletic Commission)

THIS AGREEMENT made and entered into this ____1st____ day of ____Sept.____ 19 **59**

between the **Micheal S. Jacobs & Jake Mints promotion** Club of the City of ____**Pittsburgh**____ and

Commonwealth of Pennsylvania, a duly licensed Boxing Club under the laws of the Commonwealth of Pennsylvania;

party of the first part, and ____**Billy Soose**____ of the City of ____**Pittsburgh**____

and State of ____**Pa.**____, a duly licensed Boxer, License No. _____, under the laws of

the Commonwealth of Pennsylvania; party of the second part;

Witnesseth: That said party of the second part hereby agrees to enter into a Boxing Match before said club, at

its Club House, No. ____**Forbes Field**____ Street, in said City of ____**Pittsburgh**____, on the

____**25th**____ day of ____**Sept**____, 19**59**, for **8** ____ rounds, to a decision, with **Georgie**

Abrams of the City of ____**New York**____, and State of ____**N.Y.**____

as his opponent, at a weight not over **165** pounds, eight hours before the said contest, on the official scales of the

club, for which match the party of the first part agrees to pay, after said contest, and the party of the second part

agrees to accept, as in full all his claims and demands for and on account of the performance by him of this contract

the sum of ____**$750.00**____Dollars, or _____ per cent, of the gross receipts of the house and expenses as follows:

____**Two round trip tickets from New York**____

IT IS UNDERSTOOD AND AGREED that said contest shall be with gloves, as provided in Rule 2, of the Rules of the Pennsylvania State Athletic Commission, or any amendments thereto, and to be furnished by the party of the first part and shall be conducted in all respects in conformity with the Laws of the Commonwealth of Pennsylvania, and the Rules and Regulations adopted by the Athletic Commission of said Commonwealth, which are hereby made a part of this agreement. The Referee and Judges for said contest shall be persons duly licensed to act as such by the Pennsylvania State Athletic Commission, and assigned to act, as Referee and Judges by the Pennsylvania State Athletic Commission. If the said Commission shall decide that the party of the second part did not enter into this contract in good faith, or is not honestly competing, or did not honestly compete, or is guilty of an act detrimental to the interests of boxing, it is agreed that the contest shall be stopped; in which event the party of the second part shall not be entitled to the compensation above named or any part thereof, and that such decisions of the Commission shall be absolutely final and conclusive.

The party of the second part hereby agrees to deposit with the Pennsylvania State Athletic Commission, cash,

certified cheque or accepted draft for the sum of _____ dollars, as forfeit money, to guarantee his appearance, his making the weight as above agreed and for his performance of this contract in all other respects.

If said party of the second part shall fail to appear or make the weight agreed upon, or if said party is not in physical condition and should fail to pass the required examination by a duly Licensed Physician, then said forfeit money may at the discretion of the Athletic Commission be forfeited to the party of the first part and under these cir-

cumstances the party of the first part will pay to _____ the other contestant in this match, or

his duly authorized manager, the sum of _____ dollars, as liquidated damages. If for any reason other than the failure on the part of either of the two contestants to appear, the party of the first does not fulfill his contract, the party of the first part shall then pay to the party of the second part an amount equal to said forfeit as liquidated damages, unless this match is cancelled by mutual consent.

IT IS UNDERSTOOD AND AGREED that the party of the second part shall personally report at the above named place for weighing and medical examination in accordance with the Rules and Regulations of the Pennsylvania State Athletic Commission, and shall report at the club to the Promoter two hours before the time set for the contest, the default of which shall be a breach of this contract. It is also distinctly agreed that there shall be no other agreement for covering this contest than herein contained for weights or times for weighing in.

IT IS FURTHER AGREED that if said party of the second part unless into another contest prior to the one herein contracted for and is defeated, or in any other way does anything calculated to lessen his present value as an attraction, the party of the first part shall have the option to rescind and cancel this contract without further liability hereunder, provided such cancellation is approved by the Pennsylvania State Athletic Commission.

IT IS UNDERSTOOD AND AGREED that said party of the first part is to make all arrangements for said contest and to provide suitable place and proper facilities for the staging of said contest, and such conveniences and appliances as may be reasonably necessary shall be provided.

IT IS UNDERSTOOD AND AGREED that all parties to this contract hold licenses as provided for in the laws of the Commonwealth of Pennsylvania governing Boxing, and that no one shall be permitted to participate in said contest in any way who is not duly licensed.

IN WITNESS WHEREOF, the said parties hereto have hereunto set their hands and seals the day and year first above written.

In the presence of: _____

Micheal S. Jacobs & Jake Mints promotion. _____ Club

By ____Michael S Jacobs____

_____ Boxer

By ____Per JM.____ (L.S.)

_____ Manager.

This contract must be executed in triplicate, one copy to be filed with the Pennsylvania State Athletic Commission, Philadelphia, Pa., and all the conditions herein mentioned are subject to the law and rules of said Commission.

In Reply, Please Refer to
File No.

841 Clifford Davis Federal Building
Memphis, Tennessee 38103
January 27, 1987

Mr. Gene Sebastian
Civil Aviation Security Field Office
3420 Norman Barry Drive
Suite 275
Atlanta, Georgia 30354

Dear Gene:

Thank you for all your assistance in connection with planning the Command Post Exercise recently held at the Memphis International Airport. We were very sorry you were not able to be present. The three-day exercises were extremely valuable to our personnel, as well as to many other elements of the law enforcement community who would be involved in the event of a real airport emergency.

Please pass on to Vic Echevarria our appreciation of his complete cooperation. For your information, he was certainly a gentleman, completely professional in his conduct, offering excellent input into the training exercise and a valuable asset to the overall training session.

I look forward to working with you again in the future and to coordinating our needs for similar training in the Nashville area in the coming year.

Sincerely yours,

William D. Fallin
Special Agent in Charge

MOBILE AIRPORT AUTHORITY

MOBILE MUNICIPAL AIRPORT
P. O. BOX 88004
MOBILE, ALABAMA 36608-0004

June 7, 1990

AUTHORITY
MEMBERS

DUDLEY E. DAWSON, JR.
CHAIRMAN

MATTHEW S. METCALFE, JR.
VICE CHAIRMAN

THOMAS A. HORST, JR.
SECRETARY/TREASURER

CHARLES E. CHAPMAN
ASSISTANT SECRETARY/TREASURER

ARTHUR R. OUTLAW
MEMBER

Mr. Eugene A. Sebastian
Manager
Civil Aviation Security Field Office
Federal Aviation Administration
1680 Phoenix Parkway, Suite 114
College Park, GA 30349

Dear Gene:

I want to join with Chief Moore in thanking you for giving us the opportunity to play a part in the Civil Aviation Security Seminar/Crisis (Hijack)
Management Seminar here in Mobile. While other commitments precluded my
being in attendance as much as I would have liked, Chief Moore has told
me that your staff and the other participants did a great job.

I want to particularly thank Bob Cook and Chuck Brockman for their fine
administrative assistance and guidance and Gloria McMullen for the professional work she did on registration and attendant matters with the aid
of Pam Phillips.

Many good comments were heard also about the knowledge and professionalism
of TSI Instructors Jack Crawford and Darrell Weimers as well as Phil Lilly
from your Atlanta Office and luncheon speaker Randal Duncan of the FAA Drug
Investigative Support Unit. They all well deserve our plaudits.

I trust you will let all these folks know of our gratitude, and, once again,
many thanks to you for your thinking of our airport on this and other matters
of mutual interest.

Sincerely,

M. O. Burgess, Jr., A.A.E.
Director of Aviation

MOB/m

The Story of Gene Sebastian

CHAPTER TEN:

Gene Follows in his Brother's Footsteps

Youth, the Amateur Years and the War

After Billy Soose's retirement, his younger brother Gene gave boxing a shot. At the age of 15, and having spent much of his life watching his older brother in the ring, Gene Sebastian began his amateur career. His older brother never supported his younger sibling's choice of career. For Billy, boxing was a tough sport and he advised his younger brother to pursue other careers.

Home during school breaks, he told Gene of his successes but advised his sibling to attend college, but not pursue boxing. (Tennis star John McEnroe tried to discourage his younger brother Patrick from following him into professional

Tennis. While Patrick never obtained the success that his brother did, he still made a good living at the game and is now currently involved as both an announcer and the captain of the United States Davis Cup Team). In some cases, an older sibling is not always supportive of a younger sibling's choices- often due to their own negative experiences.

Interestingly, neither Billy Soose nor John McEnroe felt that their younger brothers had the skills needed to survive in their sports.) Soose knew that boxing was a tough game and that there were easier ways to make a living. Also the difference in age between the two brothers was considerable. Soose acted in some part as a father as much as an older brother.

Gene Sebastian weighed 137 pounds and had the distinct advantage of being trained by former championship boxer, Al Wolgast. Under the tutelage of Wolgast, the young Sebastian fought in many amateur events throughout Western Pennsylvania, and Eastern Ohio.

Three years after starting his amateur career, World War II was in full swing and Gene, like his older brother, enlisted in the U.S. Navy. His first tour of duty included the island of Manus in the Admiralty Islands, located in the South Pacific.

Gene maintained his Amateur career in the Navy as he continued to fight. During the War, Gene Sebastian grew into a Middleweight and found some success fighting in the service. After a dozen victories, Sebastian challenged "Iron Head" Smith, an amateur tough man for the "Middleweight Championship of the South Pacific." Sebastian represented the sailors of US Navy's ABSD#4. In a tough match, the younger Sebastian pulled out a victory against "Iron Head."

During his tour of duty, Japanese Kamikazes (suicide bombers) attacked Sebastian's ship. The ship suffered a heavy loss of life, and the times when the Japanese planes weren't attacking the ship, nature took over. Many of Gene's friends and shipmates would die while his ship was struck by Typhoons and tidal waves.

CHAPTER ELEVEN:

Gene Moves Out

Returning Home

Gene Sebastian still had boxing in his blood after the war ended, but his brother Billy continued to discourage him. Soose told his brother, "I don't want you in the ring! Only a few boxers become titleholders. The remaining fighters are still counting telephones. I don't want to see you hurt." Gene was taken aback by the former champion's response. Nor was his brother, at least outwardly, impressed with Gene's wartime boxing.

Against his brother's wishes, Gene would continue to box as an amateur, having thoughts and dreams of eventually turning pro. A number of promoters approached Gene Sebastian. At that time Gene was fighting without a contract for fight promoter Mike Polumbo. Gene again wrote to Billy, hoping for some encouragement, but Billy Soose offered none. He told his younger sibling that fight promoters "treat their fighters like pieces of meat and would only use him to better themselves."

As a fighter, Gene was considered a scrapper and one newspaper reporter wrote that, "A good scrapper, Sebastian is a crowd pleaser." In one fight with Jim Marshall, the hard battling Sebastian measured his opponent. Marshall spent most of the fight backing away, and wisely avoiding a slugfest with Sebastian. During the fight, Marshall attempted a wild haymaker right meant for the jaw; while missing badly with the punch, Marshall did a somersault. He may have amazed the crowd with his acrobatic skills, but Marshall did little to enhance his chance for a victory.

Many around Gene were convinced that he could be a contender if he turned pro. His brother Billy feared that his younger brother was being used and promoted because of his name. Many professional businessmen, and fight promoters came forward with generous offers to move Sebastian up into the professional ranks.

One of these who encouraged Gene was Bob Letera, of New Castle, PA, who had worked with such notable fighters as Jess Willard, James J. Jefferies and Johnny Kilbane. Letera, who managed Willard's tour throughout Pennsylvania, later saw Sebastian fight in New Castle, in 1947. He quickly offered him a job in the boxing game, believing that Gene had a lot of potential with his boxing abilities.

Taking advantage of the GI Bill, Gene decided to attend Westminster College in New Wilmington, PA, majoring in business administration and hotel management. But Gene still pursued his dreams of being a professional fighter. For fighting was in Gene's blood.

During the summer, Gene would train in the Pocono's, at the same place that Billy trained at, and eventually owned. A number of the other fighters that were training there with Gene told brother Bill that Gene was looking pretty good in the ring.

Billy, a bit annoyed that Gene was not taking his advice, decided to see how good Gene really was. He donned his training gear and asked to go a few rounds with Gene and two other fighters.

Soose showed no mercy to Gene, as he overwhelmed his brother with his wrath and power. In the second round, Soose landed a vicious shot that separated three ribs. The other fighters were not spared either. Soose bloodied both fighters in a display of power. It was as if for a few brief moments, the old retired champion had relived his past. As for Gene, he laid in the ring in great pain with three broken ribs. Billy's goal was to teach Gene a lesson, encouraging him to give up the sport of boxing and concentrate on earning a living in a different profession.

Gene became very angry when he learned that Billy had hurt him intentionally, and after the doctor taped him up, he packed his bags and hitchhiked home to his parents without saying goodbye. Gene was determined to prove his brother wrong. When his mother asked him about the injury, Gene, choosing not to tell her the truth, simply said that he injured himself while Billy and Gene were cutting down trees. As far as his mother was concerned, a tree had fallen down on Gene. But Gene was very stubborn, and still not discouraged enough to quit the sport. Gene Sebastian would continue to fight as an amateur throughout Western Pennsylvania and the Ohio Valley, while still attending college.

One night in Youngstown, Ohio, Gene took a pounding. This pounding was followed by a few more losses. Gene started to see the wisdom of his brother's advice. With a record of 30 wins and only seven losses, Sebastian got the message. Gene told Mike Polumbo that he had decided to follow the advice of his older brother, and that he was too light a puncher and too slow a thinker to continue in the boxing wars.

However Gene's anger with his older brother continued. In 1949 Gene decided to drop out of college and find his way in the world without boxing. Billy offered to help, but Gene steadfastly refused. The memories of three broken ribs still affected his relationship with his brother. Gene packed his bags and continued his long journey in various fields that would eventually do him honor and make Billy and the rest of his family proud.

Gene's first stop after leaving home was in Washington, D.C. where he enrolled and later graduated from the Lewis Hotel Training Institute. After graduation he quickly found a job at the Hamilton Hotel as a front office manager, where he often would assume the assistant manager position.

His father, Albert Sebastian, had become seriously ill in 1950. Gene returned home to Western Pennsylvania to be with him. His parents had moved to the neighboring city of Sharon, PA., where they had built the Shenango Inn, a 70-room hotel. Gene stayed and became the office manager.

Gene enjoyed this job, for many of the guests and visitors there remembered his brother's ring ability. Gene's own reputation, as a fighter was still fresh in many guests' minds as well. While Gene may not have been the fighter that his brother was, he still had a very respectable amateur career, and as often as not the guests remembered.

One gentleman who had seen Gene fight in the past was a State Police Commander, Jerry Miller, who was also the husband of Gene's former English teacher. Jerry indicated that the State Police would be very receptive to an athlete who was from the valley. Jerry Miller worked on obtaining Gene Sebastian an appointment to the Pennsylvania State Police Academy in Hershey.

At this point Gene decided for good that if he wasn't good enough to continue his hopes for a professional career in the ring, he would instead pursue a career in law enforcement, and fight crime in his native state. In 1951, Gene started his new career in law enforcement, a career that would bring him to far greater heights than those he had previously attempted. Gene no longer would follow in his brother's footsteps as a fighter, and now Gene Sebastian had moved out of his brother's large shadow altogether.

When Billy Soose returned home to Sharon for a visit with the family, he told Gene that he loved him and how proud he had made him. Since Gene had always looked up to his world champion brother, those words hit home hard. Whatever rift that had existed between them from those three broken ribs had healed.

CHAPTER TWELVE:

The Start of his Law Enforcement Career

Gene served six years (1951-1957) with the Pennsylvania State Police, and during that time met and fell in love with Helen Mae Bloom, who was home for summer vacation from school. Mae helped in her parents' dry cleaning plant (Gene joked with us, "no, it wasn't a doughnut store") in between her college breaks.

Gene had been stationed at the Meadville Substation and was investigating a burglary at the dry cleaning plant, where he met Mae, and it was love at first sight. They wed after an eight-month courtship. The wedding was held in a small Methodist Church in Saegerstown, PA. This marriage is still strong after more than a half century.

Most of Gene's assignments at the time involved illegal gambling, dismantling whiskey stills, drug enforcement, and investigating traffic deaths. One of State Trooper Sebastian's more dangerous assignments was a time when a 40-year-old drunken male barricaded himself in his home, holding his six children as hostages. This crazed person had already shot and wounded several Constables.

Gene and other troopers arrived on the scene, while the hostage taker was continuing to make threats to kill the children, as well as all of the officers now on the scene. Gene physically broke into the house and negotiated with the hostage taker for about 35 minutes before this man surrendered, perhaps saving many more lives and preventing many more injuries.

There were many other tense moments for Gene as a police officer. He had to smash some moonshine operations, make drug arrests and on one occasion had to deal with some insane escapees. On one occasion he helped quell the Penn State Penitentiary riots.

In Gene's work, he did security during the breaking of the Flight Engineers Union. Gene's criminal investigations included dealing with blackmail, baggage thefts, fraudulent checks, stolen credit cards and hijacking, including Eastern Air Lines flights to Cuba.

During his time as a Pennsylvania trooper, his wife Mae gave birth to a beautiful daughter, Dara Lee, and two years later to a son, Scott. With his background in law enforcement growing, Gene felt that there were many other ways to further his career in his now chosen profession. So after six years with the Pennsylvania State Troopers, he left (1957), and took a position in Miami, Fla., with Eastern Air Lines, as their security investigator, reporting directly to the airline President Eddie Rickenbacker, and his Security Director Sal Minisalle.

CHAPTER THIRTEEN:

Eastern Airline Security: A New Step

In 1963, in Miami, Fla., while working for Eastern Airlines, Gene was called to a customer counter, where he had to deal with a very difficult customer. The customer turned out to be the former World Heavyweight champion Rocky Marciano. Marciano was on his way to Boston and didn't have enough cash on hand to cover the price of the ticket. He promised that he would pay the bill when he arrived at his destination. This was not the normal way that an airline conducts their business. Gene introduced himself to Marciano, as Billy Soose's brother, and after a brief conversation with Rocky, allowed him to board the plane. True to his word, the bill for that trip was paid almost immediately after Rocky arrived, and Gene would never hear of Marciano falling behind on his bill payments to Eastern Airlines again.

Gene left Eastern and the warmth of Florida for a new position in 1965 with Northeast Air Lines. He remained with Northeast Air Lines, in charge of internal, criminal and physical security investigations until their merger with Delta Air Lines in 1971. When living in Florida, his wife Mae gave birth to their second daughter, Lisa Joy.

Shortly after that birth and gaining the respect of top level personnel in the airline industry, Gene was asked to consider a new position with Northeast Air Lines, this time as their Corporate Security Director of Investigations, based in Boston, Mass.

Among his adventures was one dealing with a plane crash on Moose Mountain, in New England, where only 10 of the 44 passengers on board would survive. Gene also was placed in charge of handling security cuts and investigating fraud losses.

Hijackings and terrorist attacks were beginning to enter Gene's mind. In 1971, he wrote the following: "The award winning novel, 'Airport' portrayed the ease with which a would-be world traveler could board an airline for any selected destination without the benefit of a properly purchased ticket."

Joining the FAA

With his extensive background and experience in Police Administration and Air Security Management, the Federal Aviation Administration offered Gene Sebastian a position with the Federal Aviation Administration as a Field Chief.

His many duties in that capacity, included representing the Agency in eleven foreign countries. Gene met with the Cabinet Ministry of Transportation, Finance, Airports and Defense, to discuss the International Civil Aviation Organization (ICAO) treaty requirements. Sebastian would evaluate the operations, and reported those findings to the United States Ambassadors of the Countries he served.

In many of the Communist countries, Gene was considered to be a marked man. The US Ambassador to these Countries instructed him that no matter what happens, do not do anything to embarrass America, and Gene willingly complied.

One of his assignments led him to Hungary, the birthplace of his father. In 1985, Congress passed a law requiring that foreign airports meet basic standards in regard to security. Gene's goal was to ensure that the Budapest airport met the standards. Sebastian told us that a failure to comply meant that the airport would be closed to American commerce.

When Gene Sebastian came off the plane, The American council from the American Embassy briefed him. Gene remembered that he was never alone when he walked on Hungarian soil, and the American Embassy warned him that KGB officials could examine his luggage or his hotel room with no provocation. "I was told that if I saw Hungarian or KGB officials examining my room,

I was to allow them to continue. I was not to resist under any circumstances," Gene said.

For five days, Sebastian worked with the Hungarian Ministry of Defense, and the Ministry of Labor. "Any mistake on my part and I could be locked up in their prison and there were no guarantees that the United States government could do much to help, so I had to be very careful," Gene recalled.

However as the days went by, Gene went on with his job. He remembered that his father would tell him that the Hungarian people were openly warm and friendly, but in 1986 he saw nothing but sadness in the Hungarians that he met. There was no evidence of the friendliness that his father had told him about. Many of the Hungarian officials were apprehensive of this mission and the fact that Gene spoke Hungarian. (Tom Donelson's wife observed that when his wife visited Russia during the cold war as part of her Russian studies, Russians feared any American who could speak the Russian language. She was told not to openly speak Russian or let it be known that she understood the language. Whether the apprehensiveness of the Hungarian officials was due to Gene's understanding of their language and culture, or to his assignment, we may never know.)

By day four, his hosts shared Vodka with him and as he prepared to leave; one Hungarian official kissed him on the cheek. Years later, Gene Sebastian would meet with members of the Hungarian boxing team at the 1996 Summer Olympics. During those games, he worked as a boxing official. And, during these games, the friendliness that his father told him about was finally seen in the eyes of those boxers. Gene felt that during his trip to 1986, he saw the results of the oppressive nature of the government and its effect on the people. Those fighters in 1996 were no longer living under a communist regime.

As part of his duties, Gene Sebastian become one of the original 20 Federal Air Marshals, and served the Government in that capacity from 1971 -1981. He received his training for this post at the Border Patrol Academy in Brownsville, TX.

His training included a stint at the FBI National Academy in Quantico, VA, as well as the Federal Law Enforcement Training Center in Brunswick, Georgia. Gene was ready to continue his service to America.

The authority to create the Federal Air Marshal program derived from the Federal Aviation Act of 1958, and International Security and Development Cooperation of 1985 added additional powers. "As a Federal Air Marshall I endured 11 weeks of rugged basic training, that included strenuous physical requirements, management of hostage situations, and a number of simulated exercises involving bombs, hand grenades, and terrorist acts aboard a large aircraft," Gene said of his training.

As Gene mentioned, being an Air Marshall can be one of the most boring things you can do. You just sit on the plane and wait. It's far from a glamorous job. Because of the air marshal program, Gene had been trained to handle (fly) a plane in case something would happen to the pilot, as it did on Sept. 11. Even today, Gene considers terrorists as sworn enemies of the civilized world, and sadly on that fateful day of the World Trade Center disaster, there were only a limited number of federal air marshals on duty, throughout the entire United States.

Among Gene's assignments was the transportation of political refugees from the Muriel Boat Lift, when Fidel Castro released thousands of jailed Cuban prisoners, to various parts of America in 1980. Among Gene's responsibilities was to release Cubans to sponsors or turn the criminals over to prison authorities. Gene remembered that many Floridian Cubans would send money to ensure that family members would come out during the boatlift. But many of these Cubans saw their money slip into the pockets of Cuban officials without gaining their relatives freedom.

Nearly 125,000 Cubans had to be dealt with, and Gene spent nearly four months helping to place those Cubans with willing sponsors.

Gene investigated the bombing of a TWA flight that exploded in flight from Rome to Athens.

Among the people he worked with was the Italian Ambassador, in regard to the explosion.

Gene Sebastian was and remains clearly a man ahead of the times, at least ten years ahead. He stated to one of the authors, "In the early 1970's, for example, we revolutionized the Civil Aviation Security System by instituting a sky marshal program and by implementing a highly effective passenger screening system designed to stem the wave of hijackings experienced at that time. But as the level and nature of threat to the traveling public has continuously varied, so has our response."

Gene's department was established in 1971, during the 'homesick Cuban hijacking syndrome'. The hijacking graduated to the extortionist – the D.B. Cooper incident - parachuting from a Northwest Airlines aircraft near Seattle, WA., to international terrorism- or like the bombing of Pan Am flight #103, in Scotland, by terrorists in 1988. While many believe that war on terror began on September 11, 2001, the bomb that tore through Pan Am Flight #103 put the lie to those thoughts. Gene and his follow Air Marshals were ground soldiers in an unknown war being fought. Terrorists declared war on the United States long before they struck on our soil on September 11th..

From 1961 when the hijackings first began, thru 1971, U.S. aircraft (78) and 10 general aviation aircraft were successfully commandeered. Of that total, 80 hijacked flights were diverted to Cuba and eight to other countries. The responsible people involved were alleged to have been homesick Cubans who simply wanted to return to their native land.

Hijacking graduated from the homesick Cuban to the extortionists. Reference the D.B. Cooper event case files whereby the criminal involved hijacked a Northwest flight, demanded and received large sums of money and then parachuted out of the aircraft over rugged northwest mountain terrain of our country. And now we move forward to acts of terrorism.

In 1986, Gene transferred to the Southern Regional office of the FAA, and after undergoing open-heart surgery in 1995, retired from his position after receiving numerous awards in recognition of his many accomplishments to his Country, the FBI, FAA and the aviation community. His last career position was as a Judicial Court Bailiff to the Honorable State Court Judge, Morris Braswell. The Judge was a man that Gene highly respected. Braswell, when on the bench or in his chambers always had compassion for those individuals that were brought before him.

When asked his views on the present war on terror, he remarked, "Terrorists are enemies of the civilized world who seek to spread fear, chaos, and destruction. They have no regard for innocent life and they cast themselves as warriors who will change the world...Only severe punishment would deter those murderers who have no conscience." Gene told us that since 9/11, the Federal Air Marshall Program has been rebuilt to face the new threats, and the number of new Air Marshals has not been released for obvious reasons.

CHAPTER FOURTEEN:

Retirement

But the word retirement didn't sit well with Gene Sebastian. Even with his ongoing health problems, he was never the type of person to be idle. So when Buddy Davis, President of Georgia Amateur Boxing asked him for help, Gene was right there. He became an amateur boxing official, deciding to give back to the sport he had loved for so long, and that his brother Billy had excelled in. He also continued to accept public speaking invitations to talk on the subject of terrorism.

Gene still loved boxing and became Chief Official for USA Boxing in Georgia, assisted by his very capable son Scott. Scott fought in New England as an amateur in the welterweight class and had won the New England Golden Gloves title in 1974.

Like his Uncle Billy Soose and his father Gene, Scott was both a talented and gifted fighter. He never turned pro, but rather chose to study the science of boxing and become involved as an amateur referee and later trainer. Scott attended Gene's induction into the Tennessee, Alabama, Georgia (T.A.G.) Hall of Fame, where he was honored for his commitment to USA boxing. Presently Scott trains fifteen fighters, both professional and amateurs.

In June 2000, Gene accepted a post as ring official for the North American Boxing Federation (NABF), and the same year he was appointed a ring official for the Georgia State Boxing Commission, reporting directly to Executive Director Tom Mishou. And despite his continuing failing health, Gene continued to referee and judge every amateur boxing event in the State.

Sports writer Wally Wachter wrote: "Sebastian brings a wealth of pugilistic know-how to refereeing. He was an amateur champion in his hometown of Farrell, and had great success in many fights in Western Pennsylvania and Eastern Ohio."

Gene's philosophy on amateur boxing should be a lesson to all. "I think the biggest problem is that these coaches throw these kids in the ring before they are ready. That does them no good. They need to learn to box, not just walk in the ring and swing wild. That's the beauty of boxing and a lot of people have gotten away from teaching it."

Gene's philosophy of teaching has reached out to a new generation of Sebastians. His son, Scott, runs a gym in Atlanta, Georgia and has 15 fighters under his wing.

Scott grew up in the world of boxing, listening to the stories of his father's and uncle's exploits. One of the first fights that he attended was the Cassius Clay-Sonny Liston fight in Miami when Clay stunned the world and upset the Heavyweight champion. (Shortly afterwards, Clay would change his name to Muhammad Ali.)

Scott started boxing at the age of 14 but never pursued a professional career. He stayed in the game as a boxing writer for magazines and websites. He followed in his father's footsteps and became a boxing official which included involvement with USA Boxing. His love for boxing never waned, and he decided to open his own gym at the age of 45. His goal is to produce a world champion.

Scott, like his father, has dedicated much of his time to seeing that his uncle inducted in the International Boxing Hall of Fame. "If Don King can be inducted, my uncle certainly should be," Scott quipped to a newspaper reporter. When asked why run a boxing gym? Scott answered, "It always came back to the advice, 'do what you love, do what you feel passionate about.'" For Scott, after over two decades in the private sector, he returned to the family business- boxing.

As Scott returns to the sport that made his uncle a household word in the late 30's and early 40's, there is one irony. His uncle walked away from the sport after his days in the ring were over. For Billy Soose, he had entered into the business world and would never looked back. His brother

Gene and nephew Scott re-entered the sport they loved later in life. Gene stated, "I had gotten away from boxing until my son became involved." Both Gene and Scott became boxing officials and now Scott is a manager and trainer of young talent. He is filling a role for many young boxers that Paul Moss filled for Billy Soose. The cycle has now come full circle.

CHAPTER FIFTEEN:

Billy's Final Journey and Recollections

In 1994, Billy Soose contacted his younger brother Gene and asked him to accompany him to his (Billy's) induction into the World Boxing Hall of Fame in Los Angeles, which he proudly did.. At the time Bill was divorced and had two daughters. Gene, along with his wife Mae, and children visited with Bill at least once a year. The children adored their Uncle Billy and Mae thought very highly of Gene's older brother.

There they spent many days reminiscing about the past, as loving brothers who had a great amount of respect and admiration for each other generally do. "Billy was always there to listen to my journeys and experiences throughout my career in law enforcement and corporate security," Gene recalls.

In the summer of 1998, Billy Soose's health took a turn for the worse, while vacationing and playing golf in Naples, FL. Everyone knew that the former world champion lived on borrowed time. Gene first traveled to Florida, where the doctor told him that Billy was refusing to take his medication, and without it, there was little anyone could do. The doctor said that 'without his medication, Billy Soose wouldn't get as far as the hospital parking lot'.

Billy returned with his brother to Gene's home in Fayetteville, GA., to recover and regain some of his strength. He improved enough in a few weeks to return to his home in his beloved Pocono Mountains.

Billy returned home to the Pocono's where he was going to live out the final days of his life by himself. Gene visited with him there also, but Billy, stubborn to the very end, just didn't want to take his medication. Gene recalls: "The doctors had told us that if he continued to be that stubborn, he would soon die".

When Gene visited Bill in late summer of 1998, he found him, not unexpectedly, in failing health. When he returned to Georgia and his wife and family, he knew that he would never see his older brother alive again. On September 5,1998, one of Bill's golfing buddies called Gene with the tragic, yet not unexpected news that his brother, former great middleweight champion of the world, Billy Soose had died.

As expected, no matter how much you accept that death is inevitable, it is almost always taken hard, and Gene took it very hard. Choked up, Gene then talked to his pastor and Billy's former wife Peggy about arrangements for the funeral service.

Gene Sebastian always credited his successes to his wife Mae, who stood by his side. She allowed him, without complaining, to serve his Country and follow his dreams to travel at length in carrying out his assignments with the Federal Government.

Billy Soose's final and only request of his younger sibling was to ask Gene to help close out his illustrious boxing career, and help him become enshrined as a member of the International Boxing Hall of Fame in Canastota, NY.; a request that so far has been snubbed by the Hall of Fame. Gene and his son Scott have taken up the good cause, as Billy was certainly not only one of the greatest middleweights of the 20th Century, but was also a humanitarian, setting up a $25,000 boxing scholarship fund at Penn State University.

Gene simply states: "With his family's love and with the Lord's blessing, Whom is always in my corner, I simply can't fail and will continue to fight on. My brother Billy Soose will, sooner or later, be inducted into the International Boxing Hall of Fame"

Presently, Gene suffers from congestive heart failure. Gene stated that his wife and children aided his recovery during his hospital stay from heart by-pass surgery, as well as during his present coronary artery and damaged heart condition. Despite his own failing health, Gene's life mission is simple, to get his brother, Billy Soose, the champion that time has seemed to forget, his deserved place in boxing's most sacred cathedral, the International Boxing Hall of Fame.

Epilogue

Presently, Gene and Scott Sebastian work hard to get Billy Soose inducted into the International Boxing Hall of Fame. We joined the effort as well. We have already made the case that Soose deserves to be part of the International Boxing Hall of Fame designation. He fought the best of his generation and beat most of them. It was his service to his country that shortened his career. What if Soose fought three or four more years? Soose was one of the best middleweights and was well on his way to becoming one of the best light heavyweights.

As for Gene, his journey took a different direction. For many years, Gene Sebastian stood on the rampart of the war on terror; an unknown soldier in what was for many years an unknown war, fighting an unseen enemy. Both men were heroes in their own right, and now Gene is committed to one cause- to see his brother's outstanding ring prowess recognized.

The authors of this book join them in fighting the good fight. Billy Soose deserves to be enshrined in the International Boxing Hall of Fame.